The General Care and Maintenance of
Popular Monitors
and Tegus

WITI

Michael Bal

The Herpetocultural Library®

AdvANCEd
VivARiUM
SYSTEMS, inc.

10728 PROSPECT AVE. SUITE G
SANTEE, CA 92071-4558 USA

Library of Congress Catalog Card Number: 96–183295

ISBN 1-882770390

PRINTED AND BOUND IN THE UNITED STATES OF AMERICA.

Cover photography by Jeff Littlejohn.
Design and layout by Bridget M. Pilcher.

*For Barbara, whose devotion to my animals virtually rivals my own,
and
for the "Goofster," the "tamest" savannah monitor I have ever had the
privilege of having for a "pet."*

Acknowledgements

The author would like to thank Chris Estep, Glen Carlzen, Robert Mailloux, Ned and Edward Gilmore, Greg Naclerio, and Mark Bayless for their support and photographic contributions.

Contents

Foreword

During the four-plus years since the original edition of this book appeared, much has been published concerning monitors. A symposium devoted entirely to "monitor research" (Böhme and Horn 1991) was issued, and an obscure little atlas devoted to varanid anatomy (Surahya 1989) has come to my attention. Auffenberg (1994) published a third volume about monitors, and Harold Cogger (1992) has issued a new edition of his excellent work about Australia's herpetofauna. Finally, a wonderful little volume about varanids was written by Brian Green and Dennis King (1993), and Robert Sprackland published a beautifully illustrated work called *Giant Lizards* (1992), one–third of which is devoted to monitor lizards. All of these books should be of great significance to anyone curious about these marvelous lizards, and they will be pleased to discover that interest has truly taken off. In addition, the organization known as Varanix has become immensely successful, and its publication, *VaraNews*, now in its fourth year, has recently been issued in an improved and expanded format. Yet despite the appearance of all these useful publications, little has appeared that is entirely devoted to the captive care of these lizards. Thus, Advanced Vivarium Systems and I concluded that an expanded edition of this book was needed. We chose to use color photographs to enhance the text as well. We have expanded coverage in this edition to include some material about Tegus because their captive care is similar to monitors and because they reach similar sizes. Brief descriptions have also been added to cover several additional species of monitors that have become somewhat generally available since this book was first published.

I thank all the numerous readers and users of the first edition (especially those on Internet's rec.pets.herp) for their kind words and encouragement, and I pray that they will find this new edition as serviceable as the earlier one. I also thank Philippe de Vosjoli for his continuing faith in this project and for requesting a new revision of this book. I also acknowledge the continuing indispensable assistance of Mark Bayless and Pete Strimple for suggesting and supplying some difficult to obtain references and for agreeing, along with Dr. Kevin Wright, to help review the contents prior to publication; thanks guys for a wonderful job! Please note, however, that any errors that may have crept into the final manuscript are the sole responsibility of the author. Finally, I acknowledge Barbara Zolotorow for her inexhaustible support and encouragement

Mike Balsai

Introduction

Monitor lizards are among the largest, most active, and most intelligent of all the living species of squamate reptiles (i.e., lizards and snakes). Unfortunately, 4 of the 40 or so species of monitors (Green and King 1993) are already classified by CITES (Convention on International Trade in Endangered Species of Wild Fauna and Flora) under Appendix I (endangered), and all the rest are listed under Appendix II (50 CFR 23.23 1984). This means that they are threatened and could become vulnerable if the trade in these species is not regulated. Because of their large size, monitor lizards (particularly, though not exclusively, savannah monitors, Nile monitors, and Asian water monitors) figure prominently in the reptile leather trade (Luxmoore et al. 1988; Luxmoore and Groombridge 1989). As a side business, certain parts of their bodies are utilized to produce "exotic" souvenirs (such as their feet for key-rings [pers. observ.]). Several monitor species also serve as a source of food in their countries of origin (Luxmoore et al. 1988). Monitor lizards are fairly popular in the pet trade because of their large size, their often exquisite color patterns, their intelligence, the relative ease of their maintenance, and possibly, their alleged "dinosaur-like" and impressive appearance. Finally, it is probably no exaggeration to point out that the greatest threat to the continued existence of these lizards is the rapid disappearance of their habitats due to human encroachment (Luxmoore et al. 1988; Luxmoore and Groombridge 1989; Erdelen 1991).

The ruthless exploitation of many monitor species is causing their populations to decline. The availability of certain species, especially the Asian ones, has become dramatically reduced. In fact, the general rarity of monitors and pythons in certain parts of Asia has been implicated for the dramatic rise of rodent pest problems in these areas! The three sub-Saharan African species, however, are still available in reasonable numbers, but changing awareness toward the wildlife of Africa, coupled with the political instability in many of their countries, may change this in the future. Green and King (1993) suggested that heavy exploitation of African monitors for the "fashion industry" may bring about local extinctions. Captive breeding of monitor lizards is not common due to its relative difficulty, but progress continues to be made. Presently, though, the majority of specimens sold in the pet trade are wild-collected/imported animals (there are occasional exceptions).

Probably, the most popular and readily obtainable species of monitor is the savannah monitor *(Varanus exanthematicus)*, from Africa. Their popularity stems from the fact that they usually tame very well and do not reach the huge sizes of some of the other species. They are also, seemingly, the least expensive of all the monitors currently sold in the trade. A few other species can presently be obtained as well, and, of these, two other African species, the Nile monitor *(V. niloticus)* and the white–throated monitor *(V. albigularis)*, appear most commonly and are also relatively inexpensive. This book was written to provide essential information on the responsible husbandry of the savannah monitor and other monitor species regularly offered in the pet trade.

General Information

Monitors are moderate- to large-sized lizards belonging to the genus *Varanus* within the family Varanidae. Their closest living relatives are the helodermatids (Gila monsters and Mexican beaded lizards) and an extremely rare, obscure animal called the Bornean earless lizard, *Lanthanotus borneensis* (Estes et al. 1988). Many herpetologists also believe that monitors and their kin may be the closest lizard relatives of snakes. Some obvious characteristics of monitors include long, slender, deeply forked tongues; sharp (usually) fang-like, compressed teeth; (usually) long necks with fairly short bodies; large eyes with round pupils; moderately large, deeply inset ear openings; long heads with pointed snouts (usually); five-toed feet with large, sharp, recurved claws; long, muscular, nonbreakable tails; and the absence, for many species, of femoral pores and anal glands (Halliday and Adler 1986).

Distribution and Size

There are approximately 45 or so, living species of monitors, and of these, two-thirds are natives of Australia (Green and King 1993). The other one-third range through Africa, tropical Asia, the Middle East, and certain Pacific Islands. Although several Austra-

▲ *An adult white-throated monitor* (Varanus albigularis). *It has recently been widely accepted that this former subspecies of the savannah monitor be given full species status as* Varanus albigularis. *Photo by Glen Carlzen.*

lian species only reach a total length (TL) of 8 to 12 in. (20 to 30 cm), most species have an average TL of 3 ft or more (1 m or more) (Green and King 1993), making them the largest of all the living lizards. Monitors are completely predatory with the exception of one species from the Philippines called Gray's monitor *(V. olivaceus,* formerly *V. grayi),* which is omnivorous and is known to devour fruits and seeds, along with small vertebrates, eggs, snails, and insects (Auffenberg 1988; Card 1994b, 1995b,c). The emerald tree monitor *(V. prasinus)* may also eat fruit as captives (Sprackland 1991b, 1992), and captive savannah *(V. exanthematicus)* and white-throated *(V. albigularis)* monitors have been observed eating bananas (Bayless, pers. comm.).

The Savannah Monitor: General Information

What's in a Name?

Varanus is a late Latin term derived from the Arabic Waran which literally means monitor lizard (Gotch 1986). The name "monitor" is believed to originate from an ancient superstitious belief that these lizards would give a warning when crocodiles were nearby (perhaps because Nile monitors are often seen about crocodile nests, foraging for the eggs). The species epithet *exanthematicus* is derived from the Greek word *exanthema* which means eruption and refers to any eruptions or pimples caused by disease (Brown 1956). When applied to savannah monitors, it apparently refers to the rather large pimple-like scales on the back of the neck.

Subspecies and Distribution

In 1942, Mertens categorized four subspecies of the African savannah monitor that were, until recently, recognized as valid. They are *V. exanthematicus albigularis*, *V. e. angolensis*, *V. e. exanthematicus*, and *V. e. microstictus*. Mertens distinguished these subspecies by variations in the number of scales around the body and by variations in the number of ventral scale rows extending from the gular (throat) fold to the cloacal area. In addition, these subspecies usually differ in color.

Savannah Monitor

The subspecies most commonly seen in pet stores is *V. e. exanthematicus*. This form averages about 2.5 to 3 ft (about 1 m) TL and tends to be grayish-tan in color with fairly large light-gray (sometimes light-blue) spots with dark-brown borders along the back and sides. It ranges from Senegal in the west, to Eritrea in the east, to the Adrar mountains and the Sahara in the north, to the rain forests of the southwest.

Cape or White-throated Monitor

The subspecies Mertens named *V. e. albigularis*, the so-called Cape or white-throated monitor, is now considered a full species (*V. albigularis*) by most experts. I have found no report of any savannah monitor (*V. exanthematicus*) attempting to breed or successfully cross-breeding with the Cape monitor, and examination of the hemipenes of these two species shows them to appear quite different (see: Branch 1982; Böhme 1988; Böhme et al. 1989). The Cape monitor has a somewhat shorter, blunter snout than the Savannah monitor, the top of the head and neck are dark brown, and the back is a dark gray–brown. The cape monitor is also patterned with five to six rows of pale-yellow, dark-bordered, blotchy spots. The limbs are spotted with pale yellow, and the tail has an alternating pattern of dark-brown and off-white bands. The belly is dirty yellow, with some spotting, and can be more colorful than the pale-whitish or tannish belly of the savannah monitor.

Although the Cape monitor is considered more attractively colored than the savannah monitor by many herpetoculturists, it is rumored to have a somewhat nastier temperament. The cape monitor also reaches a larger size (5 to 6 ft [1.5 to 1.8 m]) than the savannah monitor (averages about 2 to 3 ft [about 0.6 to 1.0 m] though a large one can average about 3

to 4 ft [about 1.0 to 1.5 m]). The Cape monitor ranges from Zimbabwe and Botswana in the north, Namibia in the west, Mozambique in the east, down into South Africa. *Varanus e. angolensis* (perhaps now more correctly named *V. albigularis angolensis*, but Sprackland [1992] notes that this subspecies name has been "suppressed") shows some minor scale variation with respect to *V. albigularis*, but is otherwise similar. It ranges from Angola, north into Zaire. Both *V. albigularis* and *V. e. angolensis* attain total lengths that range from about 3.9 ft (1.1 m) to a bit over 4.3 ft (1.3 m) (although there are reports of *V. albigularis* reaching lengths of 6.6 ft [2 m]). Due to its similarity of habit and appearance, I propose that for the purposes of husbandry and care, the Cape monitor can be kept virtually identically to *V. exanthematicus* and, except where otherwise noted, the name "savannah" monitor can be taken to refer to any of the variants of *V. exanthematicus* and *V. albigularis* (however, Bayless [pers. comm.] claims that *V. albigularis* is more likely to climb than *V. exanthematicus*).

▲ *This Savannah monitor* (Varanus exanthematicus) *is displaying a threat posture. Bites from these lizards can be severe, can become infected easily, and sometimes require stitches! So handle them with care and respect. Photo by Paul Freed.*

9

Varanus e. microstictus is similar in length to *V. e. exanthematicus*, about 4 ft (1.5 m) TL, but the overall body color is darker than *V. e. exanthematicus*. It has large, very light-colored, almost squarish spots with dark borders. It ranges throughout most of eastern Africa, from Ethiopia and Somalia in the north to Kenya in the south. Sprackland (1992) noted that the validity of this subspecies is presently questioned, and this subspecies now seems to be considered by most as a subspecies of *V. albigularis (V. a. microstictus)*.

In 1964, another subspecies was proposed, called *V. e. ionidesi*, which is presumed to hail from Tanzania. Most authorities, however, believe it to be a form of *V. a. microstictus. Varanus e. ionidesi* is distinguished mostly in terms of a supposedly distinctive immature coloration, which vaguely resembles that of a juvenile *V. albigularis*. It probably is not a "true" subspecies and, more likely, it reflects a local color morph. I was told (Bayless, pers. comm.) that Laurent, the original proponent of this name, has now retracted it (Sprackland [1992] noted that the taxonomic recognition of this so-called subspecies is now "suppressed").

It is of interest to note the origin of the vast majority of "savannah" monitors sold in the pet trade. Ghana, Kenya, Togo, and Tanzania are the major sources, with supposedly 90% coming from Togo (*V. albigularis* is not found here). Ghana (*V. albigularis* is not found here) accounts for about 9%, and the remaining 1% come from Kenya and Tanzania (Bayless 1991; Luxmoore et al. 1988). Bayless (1991) reported that although *V. albigularis* is protected in the Republic of South Africa, export of "captive-born" individuals to the USA is allowed. Zimbabwe allows some export of "captive-bred" reptiles, including *V. albigularis*, and this species is exported in small numbers from Tanzania (Bayless 1991). At this writing it has not been reported exactly how these countries account for "captive born" and "captive bred" for the purposes of allowing export.

Sexing, Growth and Longevity

Sexing savannah monitors (or any monitor) is a tricky business. Like all lizards (and all squamates for that matter), male monitors have paired hemipenes, but any examination for distinguishing external characteristics will be inconclusive. Savannah monitors (as do at least a few other monitor species) also seem to have an unusual sex chromosome heteromorphism (King and King 1975; Olmo 1986; Greer 1989), but genetic testing is not an option for most herpetoculturists. Inducing the eversion of the hemipenes in full-grown monitor lizards is a difficult procedure at best, albeit males often will briefly evert these organs after defecation (beware of confusion with large cloacal glands, which sometimes evert in defecating females [Card 1995]). Herpetoculturists have sometimes resorted to probing and manually everting the hemipenes in juveniles with varying degrees of success or reliability. Card (1994), however, notes the great unreliability of this method. Relying on aggressive or submissive behaviors is also undependable. Card (1994) reported that a presumed "pair" of perenties (*V. giganteus*) at the Dallas Zoo actually turned out to be two males!

Recently, a method has been introduced that will cause the eversion of hemipenes following the injection of sterile saline (either physiological saline or lactated Ringer's solution) into the tail (see Stewart 1989). I believe this technique entails some risk to the animal and should never be attempted without the assistance of a qualified veterinarian. In addition, this procedure has been termed "unreliable" and "potentially harmful" (Card 1994a, 1995c). Another means for discerning the sex of monitors that requires the assistance of a vet, is the use of endoscopy (see Schildger 1987; Schildger and Wicker, 1992). This method is also somewhat "invasive," and risks must be weighed, including the sanitary conditions in which the animal lives. Along similar lines, fiber-optic laparoscopy has been very successfully used to sex Dumeril's monitors (Davis and Phillips 1991). Card (1994a) reported a method where measurements of the sexually dimorphic pelves of these lizards can be used; however, a drawback is the need for very accurate measurements of the ischium. Presumably, this method is derived via the measurements of these bones from radiographs as they were for helodermatids (Card and Mehaffey 1994). Hairston and Burchfield (1992) claim that sexing "well-proportioned" monitors is not too difficult, one merely looks for the hemipenal bulges in the males (at least in water monitors). They did note that these can be confused with large "scent glands" in the females and can appear almost invisible if the tails store too much fat (Hairston and Burchfield 1992). In fact, as if things were not complicated enough, Böhme (1995) showed that female monitors have paired structures that are evertible and erectile in the same area as the hemipenes of the males and that these are "miniaturized mirror images of the hemipenes of the males" (Böhme 1995, p. 129). These organs contain all the anatomical elements that are also characteristics for hemipenes for their respective males and these include such attributes as: supporting ossifications, epidermal flounces, etc. Böhme (1995) proposed that these structures be called hemiclitorii and he suspects they may be present in other lizard families (maybe all of them) as well.

The San Diego Zoo attempted to determine the sex of two Komodo monitors by testing their blood for testosterone (male hormone) levels. John Weigel (1988) suggested subjecting monitor lizards to radiographic (X-ray) analysis for sex determination, presumably because at least some of the varanid species have small bones (seen as two or sometimes three mineralized structures in the retracted hemipenis [Shea and Reddacliff 1986; Greer 1989; Card 1995c; Card and Kluge 1995]). This method has been used with great success at the Dallas Zoo (Card and Mehaffet 1994; Card and Kluge 1995). Unfortunately, savannah monitors lack such ossifications (as

do black rough-necked monitors, Asian water monitors, and Timor monitors, among the species discussed in this book). It is not known at exactly what age these ossifications can be detected in most of those species (except Gould's monitors [Card 1994a,b, 1995a; Card and Kluge 1995] that show them at about 2 years of age). A partial list of which species possess ossifications and which ones lack them is given as Table 18-3 in DeNardo (1996, p. 218).

Many reports indicate that male monitors tend to be captured much more frequently than females. Why this occurs is unknown, but it may reflect sexual differences in activity patterns (see Greer [1989] and King and Green [1993] for citations); for example, male monitors are known to patrol larger territories and are generally more active during the day than females. The size of an "average territory" for male white-throated savannah monitor lizards is

▲ *A captive-raised one-year-old savannah monitor* (Varanus e. exanthematicus) *on top of a three-year-old captive-raised male.* Photo by Chris Estep.

13

7.1 mi.^{2} [18.3 km^2] whereas for females it is 2.3 mi.^{2} [6.1 km^2], according to Alberts (1994b). Thus, if most wild-caught monitors are taken during "chance" encounters, then the most active individuals have the greatest chance of being captured (King and Green 1993). This means that a wild-caught captive monitor is statistically more likely to be male (which appears to be true [Balsai, pers. observ.] based on examination of many wild-caught specimens in the pet trade).

However, Alberts (1994b) noted that male white-throated savannah monitor lizards patrol their entire territories at only two times in the year: during the 4-month wet season (January–April) and during the 6-week mating season (July–August). During these times, males might frequently travel more than 2.5 mi. (4 km) per day! Alberts (1994b) also noted that during the rest of the year males used only a small portion of their home ranges and their daily movements were reduced. Females, on the other hand, only traversed their entire territory during the wet season and hardly moved at all during the breeding season. In fact, during this time the females stayed near their burrows and trees, apparently allowing the males to seek them out (Alberts 1994b). After the mating season, males also preferred to remain near their burrows and trees and were "alert and active in and around these refuges, but tended not to leave the immediate vicinity" (Alberts 1994b). Alberts also noted that one male remained in his tree for 73 days, moving several feet to nearby branches, but never leaving the tree. However, during the first major rainstorm of the next rainy season, this animal traveled nearly a mile to a new location where it located snails, one of its "favorite foods" (Alberts 1994b).

Breeding

Monitors, including savannahs, are considered difficult to breed as captives, though it has been done by a few zoos and individuals on various occasions, with several different species (including *V. albigularis* and *V. exanthematicus*). Certainly, most species

(except *V. acanthurus and V. tristis orientalis*) are not easily and regularly bred; at least that is the impression derived from scanning the literature. Even data about hatchlings and egg sizes are somewhat difficult to find and may often go unreported. However, "newborn" savannah monitors were recorded at an average TL of 5.4 in. (13.6 cm) and weighed 0.35 to 0.53 oz (10 to 15 g) (Roder and Horn 1994). An adult can measure over 33.4 in. (100 cm) and weigh 176+ oz (5000 g). A west African hatchling was reported to have a 5.5-in. (14 cm) TL (no weight was given). Clutch sizes range from 8 to 50 eggs, and an average derived from various reports of egg size gives a range of 1.2 in. to 1.8 in. by 0.74 in. to 0.98 in. (3.1 to 4.5 cm [length] by 1.88 to 2.5 cm [width]). Weights ranged from about 0.0032 oz to 0.14 oz (0.9 g to 4.0+ g) (Horn and Visser 1989; Sprackland 1989, 1992; Bayless and Huffaker 1992; Bayless and Reynolds 1992; Roder and Horn 1994).

▲ *A hatchling Dumeril's monitor* (Varanus dumerilii). *Photo by Glen Carlzen.*

15

▲ *This Savannah monitor* (Varanus exanthematicus) *hatchling is approximately 5 inches long. These animals will grow very fast if kept properly and will eventually require a large enclosure. Photo by Paul Freed.*

Alberts (1994b) noted that for white-throated savannah monitors found in Etosha National Park (Northern Namibia), only females above 19.7 in. (0.5 m) snout–vent length (SVL) were gravid, and no females below 17.7 in. (0.45 m) SVL produced egg clutches. Alberts concluded that these females must thus achieve some minimal body size before reproduction is possible. How this correlates with age was not reported.

The incubation periods for eggs laid by captive savannah monitors vary between 165 and 195 days (5.5 and 6.5 months) (at a temperature between 80.6°F [27°C] and 91.4°F [33°C]) whereas in the wild it may take as long as 12 months! Mating is reported to occur in August to mid-October with eggs laid in September through January and in June (Horn and Visser 1989; Sprackland 1989, 1992; Bayless and Huffaker 1992; Bayless and Reynolds 1992; Bayless 1994). Females may either dig a shallow nest for the eggs or deposit them in termite nests.

Growth

I have observed that very young savannah monitors can increase their weight as much as 5- to 10-fold in the first year and increase their length at least 2- to 2.5-fold during that time (see Horn and Visser [1991] for basic growth data for many species of monitors)! This assumes they are kept under optimal captive conditions and also depends on their feeding regimen. Since the last edition of this book (Balsai 1992), some data have appeared concerning growth rates for monitors. For example, Roder and Horn (1994) showed that their savannah monitors, on average, almost doubled in length in only 4 months and, in some cases, virtually quadrupled their weight during the same time period. Longevity of most individuals, if not all species, can be significant. Records kept on savannah monitors have shown them to reach ages of 11+ years. Other species of monitors have been recorded at ages of 15 or more years, with some of these individuals still alive when their age was noted (Bowler 1977; Slavens 1989; Slavens and Slavens 1993).

In addition, Alberts (1994b) noted large seasonal differences in body mass for both male and female white-throated savannah monitor lizards. The wet season body mass can exceed the dry season body mass by as much as 50%! Even during their inactivity as a result of cooler temperatures, the animals still lose about 4% of their body mass per month as a result of "maintenance calories" (Alberts 1994b). Males also lose body mass during the breeding season, probably due to active searching for females (Alberts 1994b).

What to Consider Before Getting a Savannah Monitor

Of the species of monitors readily available in the pet trade, savannah monitors are among the least expensive and easiest to obtain. They do not achieve the gigantic size (for lizards) that certain other species can reach, and they (particularly *V. e. exanthematicus*) generally have reliably docile dispositions. Like most reptiles, they are not especially noisy and do not demand the amount of attention that cats, dogs or birds require, nor do they cause the allergy problems that mammals and birds do. Savannah monitors feed upon whole animal foods, such as rodents (which, of course, can cause allergic reactions in some people), and need a fairly large amount of space. Remember, that the cute little lizard in the pet store that is only 7 to 8 in. (18 to 20 cm) long will grow very fast if kept properly and will eventually require a large enclosure. If the animal is flighty or aggressive it can be a bit of a challenge to handle. Also, one should be aware that little savannah monitors will grow to be large carnivorous lizards with sharp claws on powerful limbs and with sharp teeth in very strong jaws. They sometimes also use their tails as weapons. Bites from these lizards can be severe, can become infected easily, and can sometime require stitches! So handle them with care and respect.

If the above has not deterred you, then you must know that savannah monitors are intelligent (for lizards), often beautifully colored, and fascinating as vivarium subjects. These monitors are well known for usually becoming tame in captivity, with some individuals becoming almost "dog-tame." They respond to their owners to some degree and quickly learn certain routines like feeding time and cage cleaning time. The challenge of breeding these lizards should become of increasing interest to herpetoculturists, particularly when the long-term results would be a decreased demand for wild-caught specimens.

Responsible Savannah Monitor Ownership

Savannah monitor lizards are intelligent reptiles which, in captivity, have a lot of time on their hands. In no time at all, the average healthy, inquisitive monitor will be searching for a way to expand its horizons. In other words, monitors are adept at escaping improperly secured enclosures. They also have no respect whatsoever for any household objects and some love to climb. Should your pet escape, it can wreak havoc within a matter of minutes and potentially cause damage to personal property. It might even injure itself. These lizards are also good at getting into vents and between walls or into moderately large openings of any sort. If a large savannah monitor lizard escapes to the outside during the warmer weather, its perambulations and adventures can gain you (and, perhaps, indirectly, all herpetoculturists) a significant amount of notoriety. Should your pet encounter a large dog, your pet can almost certainly be injured or more likely killed. If it escapes outside in colder weather, you will definitely have a valuable and wonderful animal die from negligence.

When keeping monitor lizards, or any other large reptile for that matter, this author advocates some of the views of the board of The American Federation of Herpetoculturists (AFH). This nonprofit organization is an advocate for the interests of serious herpetoculturists while also having sensitivity for the interests of the welfare of the general public and the amphibians and reptiles themselves. The AFH emphasizes responsible herpetoculture as the foundation of its position on keeping amphibians and reptiles as captives. Recently, the AFH outlined some guidelines for the keeping of monitor lizards. These considerations are summarized in the Appendix.

What About Regulations?

As mentioned in the Appendix, there has been a trend for many cities and even states to draft various laws or ordinances to restrict or prohibit the keeping of large monitors (these also can include iguanas and tegus). Various agencies and organizations support such regulations, normally under the guise that the public needs to be protected from the "potential danger" of such animals. Most of these regulations arise from a persistent bias against reptiles which permeates the attitudes of many people concerning these wonderful animals.

▲ *Large savannah monitors can be quite a handful, but captive-raised animals tend to be docile. Agencies that aim to restrict the private ownership of savannah monitors have a biased position unsupported by statistical data. A better case could be made to ban the ownership of dogs.*
Photo by Robert Mailloux.

NONETHELESS . . .

Before purchasing any monitor lizard, "savannah" or otherwise, it would be wise to check city, state, etc. regulations for any ordinances or laws pertaining to the ownership of these lizards. Besides the various officials of the agencies involved with such enforcement, good sources of information are local herpetological organizations. It does not pay to be heedless of such laws or you could find yourself in a very unpleasant position, and you could gain a considerable amount of unwanted notoriety. If local officials contact state fish and game and/or federal fish and wildlife officers, you could be in for one of the most horrendous times of your life! In addition, your pet will probably be confiscated.

Selecting a Savannah Monitor

Selection of a lizard is a critical first step to owning a savannah monitor, and it will determine the course of your future relationship with the animal. When selecting any reptile, including a savannah monitor, choose only a healthy animal. Forget about saving any sick–looking lizard in a pet store. If a monitor looks very ill in a pet store, usually it has progressed to the point of no return, and you will almost certainly set yourself up for real disappointment. Don't waste your money and time, get a healthy animal and start off right. Be aware that the advice that follows can be reasonably applied to the purchase of any monitor species.

What to Avoid

It is generally a good idea to avoid the purchase of any aggressive adult savannah monitor (2 or more feet long). Females tend to be more aggressive, at least initially (Bayless, pers. comm.). Savannah monitors of this size are quite strong and will be a challenge to pick up and handle. Most truculent monitors will attempt to bite. Additionally, many of these initially aggressive animals will probably never become tame, even with frequent handling. It has been my experience that many such savannah monitors, though seemingly healthy looking when purchased, are in fact quite stressed. They may eventually refuse to eat, and their psychological and physiological stress will depress their immune responses (Guillette et al. 1995). When this happens, various disease symptoms may eventually become apparent, and there is a good chance the lizard may end up dying of some sickness or other.

Avoid any lizard, large or small, wild-caught or captive-born that looks unhealthy in any way. These usually refuse to eat and will look starved. They will have low body weight, will often appear dehydrated, and will generally have a "skin and bones" appearance. They often have loose skin and sunken eyes. They will seem sluggish and generally not alert. They will often be too lethargic to flick their tongues in investigation. If you are still uncertain about buying a "sick" lizard, see Barten (1992) for good reasons why you should not.

Selecting a Healthy Savannah Monitor

When available, the best choice for a savannah monitor is a captive-raised (or -born) animal which has a healthy appearance, is active and alert, and even appears a bit extroverted (not to be confused with aggressive). In this case, the size of the lizard is not too important. If it shows good health and calm behavior that is reasonably normal, it will be a good candidate as a "pet" and may even have potential for breeding. Of course, such animals should eat readily.

The second best choice is an imported young and apparently healthy savannah monitor. It should be alert, active, and in "good flesh" (i.e., a bit "chubby" but not obese). The vent/cloacal area should be clean and not have any wet or dry caked stool clinging to it. The belly should also be clean. Do not confuse normal shedding skin as a sign of bad health. The eyes should be clear. Healthy monitors readily flick their tongues both when disturbed and whenever they walk. A healthy young savannah monitor will be rather "squirmy" when picked up, but will

▲ *A hatchling Savannah monitor (Varanus exanthematicus). These monitors are among the least expensive and easiest to obtain. Photo by Bill Love.*

usually calm down with frequent handling. Very young savannah monitors will sometimes defecate when first picked up, but this unpleasant habit will usually disappear with time and frequent handling. It can be a very satisfying experience to raise a baby savannah monitor to adulthood and these will often be excellent reptile pets.

Acclimation

Acclimation (acclimatization) is when an organism becomes habituated to a different, usually abnormal, climate or environment (Lawrence 1989). It is often used to describe an animal attempting to adjust to artificial or captive conditions. Whether your newly obtained savannah monitor acclimates or not depends on its housing, maintenance, temperature, nutritional conditions, and state of health when acquired. Furthermore, an individual lizard's "psychological profile" will play a major role in its ability to acclimate.

▲ *An example of a newly imported Burundi Nile monitor which should be avoided by a prospective buyer. This animal is thin, sluggish and can barely keep its eyes open. This animal would require a certain amount of veterinary treatment to have a chance at surviving in captivity.*

When You Bring Your Monitor Home

Your monitor will need some time to adjust to its new environment. This can take a few weeks to as much as several months, and some animals will seem very stressed and may hide and fail to feed for the first few days or even weeks. Wild-caught specimens will usually puff up, hiss, and possibly swat their tails at you. Captive-raised animals usually fare better, but even they might not eat until adjusted.

Avoid moving or walking too closely and/or quickly toward the new animal or it may attempt to flee and run into the walls of its cage, possibly causing damage to its snout. It is important to provide a monitor with a shelter for hiding during this initial acclimation period and also afterward, as well. If you fail to allow the new animal to adjust, it may remain stressed. This will inhibit the immune system and, more noticeably, its appetite. Establish a regular maintenance and feeding schedule during this time. Keep as much distance between you and the animal's enclosure as possible for the first few weeks. Offer it food every 1 to 2 days, until it begins to feed regularly. Some herpetoculturists even advocate the use of an electrolyte solution like Gatorade® or Pedialite® instead of water during this period.

Within a few weeks or so, the animal should be eating regularly and gaining weight. In savannah monitors, weight loss is usually first apparent around the hips and tail. A healthy savannah monitor has a rounded tail where it joins the body, and the hips are virtually indiscernible. When the animal is eating, showing some weight gain, not appearing overly stressed, and (with nonadult animals) beginning to grow, you can work toward establishing a modicum of a pet–owner relationship.

It should be understood that a certain percentage of savannah monitors will probably not adjust well to captivity, particularly large wild-caught adults. Occasionally, with early recognition and treatment (i.e., administering electrolyte therapy, high-energy supplements, like Nutri-Cal® etc.), you may be able to revitalize them, but this can be particularly difficult if the animal is aggressive toward you. Chances

▲ *This seven year old water monitor is intelligent, friendly, and has become a wonderful animal to keep. Photo by Chris Estep.*

are that these animals will continue to be a problem and will require a considerable amount of time and effort. They will probably continue to suffer from stress and eventually, despite all your efforts, fail to thrive and die. Do not give up if you are not successful the first time, but definitely avoid purchasing sick or inactive monitors.

Feeding

Healthy savannah monitors of any size will readily feed, and it is usually a bad sign when they do not. Sometimes adults, particularly the males, will fast during their breeding season. I have also observed this to occur in some long-term captives in the late winter (January–March). If they are in good health and not thin, short fasts can be tolerated without concern, but keep a close eye on the situation, and be especially alert for dehydration.

Diets for Adult Monitors

Most adult and juvenile monitors of about 1 ft or more in total length (TL) will readily devour pre-killed rodents (all commercially bred types) or baby chickens. I have, on occasion, offered fresh fish, as well. They are also quite fond of eggs, and an occasional egg can be given, but only use egg yolks or embryonated eggs obtainable in health food markets. The whites of nonembryonated eggs contain avidin which, in excess, can induce a biotin (vitamin B_4) deficiency. This problem manifests itself as a generalized "diffuse" muscular weakness (Frye 1991). There is also a great risk of *Salmonella* infection when feeding raw eggs. A safe option is to offer cooked eggs, which eliminates both the avidin and *Salmonella*

▲ The growth rate for savannah monitors will be greatest during the first 2 to 3 years. When growth slows down it is best to reduce the feeding regimen. **See Feeding Schedules and Regimens** *section in this chapter.*

problems. Although chicken parts are also readily eaten by savannah monitors, be aware that raw chicken may also be contaminated with *Salmonella*, and is best avoided. If you do feed them chicken, make sure it has been cooked (and bear in mind that a diet heavy in chicken parts is virtually certain to be unbalanced). For an interesting general presentation of aspects of nutrition for carnivorous reptiles, the reader is referred to Allen and Oftedal (1994), Smeller et al. (1978), and Maixner et al. (1987) (and also Weldon et al. 1994; Frye 1995; Barten 1996; Donoghue and Langenberg 1996).

Monitor Diets in the Wild

It is interesting to note what these lizards eat in the wild. Losos and Greene (1988) report that the stomach contents of savannah monitors contain mostly beetles, millipedes, caterpillars, and orthopterans (grasshoppers and their relatives). Snails, centipedes, hymenopterans (ants, bees, wasps), scorpions, occasional lizard eggs, a few frogs and toads, and, most uncommonly, small lizards, baby tortoises, and small mammals make up the rest of what they report. Luxmoore et al. (1988; see also Bayless 1992b) reported that in Southern Africa their diet consists mostly of millipedes and tenebrionid beetles (darkling ground beetles). Alberts (1994b) observed that wild white-throated savannah monitor lizards living in Etosha National Park in Northern Namibia have a diet that consists mostly of land snails, various insects, and bird and reptile eggs. She also noted that because these lizards are diurnal, they rarely encounter small mammals and even more rarely consume them! She noted that at the San Diego Zoo, these lizards are fed garden snails, scrambled eggs, and ground turkey. At this zoo, these lizards achieve adult size in less than 2 years. She also cautions about the use of wild snails due to the possibility that these snails might be contaminated with pesticides. In fact, one should be aware of the dangers of using any sort of wild-caught invertebrate (including all sorts of arthropods as well as mollusks) or vertebrates (including frogs, lizards, and rodents). These dangers include the possibility of pesticide contamination, and/or the possibility that the wild-caught prey may host intermediate stages for a natural parasite of reptiles (see Rossi 1992).

Note, that diet alone is not a sole determinant for monitor lizard growth (or for any reptile, for that matter). Factors such as temperature are also very critical. As a final note, Gaulke (1991) mentioned that the ingestion of large numbers of insects by Asian water monitors *(V. salvator)* in the Philippines may actually be the result of human destruction of their habitat, limiting what they may find as available food. This is food for thought for those insisting that many monitors may largely prey upon insects in the wild.

Lemm (1994; see also Bayless 1992b) reported that he has seen more and more savannah monitors dying from "hair impactions." He also stated that many monitor keepers believe that feeding mice and rats to varanids results in obese lizards that eventually succumb to kidney failure (actually liver disease would probably be more likely if obesity is a problem). This opinion appears to be contrary to the results of studies by Smeller et al. (1978) and especially Maixner et al. (1987) and seems to be based on belief rather than experimental evidence. The most common diet I have used for nearly all monitor species has been rodents of all sizes, and fur impactions have never been observed, and that includes more than 15 savannah monitors, over the years. To be perfectly honest, I have observed impactions from rodent fur to be more common in boas than savannah monitors. Bayless (pers. comm.) reports that he has seen impactions only in very obese animals, and perhaps obesity causes problems with digestion of rodents. Obesity should not be a problem if food intake is strictly regulated and reduced if weight gain is too rapid. The problems arising from a largely rodent diet are very likely the result of overzealous feeding. I believe that many novice varanid keepers will find it much more difficult to maintain proper nutrition using a largely invertebrate diet than when using a rodent-based diet. (If an invertebrate-based diet is chosen, consult the following sources for ensuring that proper nutrition is achieved: Zwart and Rulkins 1979; Allen and Oftedal 1989; de Vosjoli 1990, 1994; McKeown 1996; Donoghue and Langenberg 1996.) Lemm (1994) also proposes that water may act as a "solvent" that breaks through fur impactions in aquatic species. I believe this to be highly speculative at best, however, and probably doubtful.

Diets for Hatchling and Small Monitors

Very young savannah monitors (i.e., under 1 ft) can be fed live crickets, earthworms ("night crawlers"), the so-called "king mealworms" (*Zophobus*) [Note: It is rumored that *Zophobus* can literally chew their way out of the bodies of lizards, therefore these larvae should probably be served prekilled. However, de Vosjoli (1990, 1994) does not mention this as a problem], and baby mice (both "pinkies" and

▲ *Prekilled mice will be readily consumed by monitors and tegus and are detected by smell.*

"fuzzies," depending on the size of your animal). In addition, I have had excellent success using canned cat food, especially poultry flavors. Use a good brand of canned cat food to ensure adequate nutrition, but remember that canned cat food should be used as a supplement (no more than two to three times per month), not as the sole diet. Use of canned cat food as a sole diet can lead to obesity and loose stools. This can normally be corrected by alternating feedings with prey animals such as fuzzies or just-weaned mice, between cat food feedings. Occasionally, canned cat food can be offered to adult monitors, especially those recovering from illness. Adult monitors, however, tend to make messes, by spreading it about the enclosure when offered canned cat food.

Size of Prey and Live Versus Prekilled Food

The size of prey that can be offered to a monitor can be judged by the size of the monitor's head and by its gape. Normally, your monitor will not attempt to devour anything it judges too large to swallow

31

▲ *Monitors on rodent diets alone will thrive if the feedings are strictly regulated to avoid obesity. Photo by Chris Estep.*

easily. For example, a hatchling savannah monitor will be unable to eat an adult mouse and will usually not attempt to do so or will cease trying very quickly. Some monitors can dismantle a large prey item with their claws and mouths and devour it in pieces, but very young animals will normally avoid doing this. There are rare times when a savannah monitor will eat a prey item that is too large, and this will usually be regurgitated sometime thereafter. This normally does not harm your animal, but monitor vomit is among the most incredibly foul-smelling materials in the world! Even a full-grown adult savannah monitor will rarely be able to eat a guinea pig or large rat (at least not without "disassembly," which can be unaesthetic and messy), but nearly any other "domesticated" rodent will be usable (e.g., prekilled hamsters, mice, gerbils, small rats, and the like). As reported above, in the wild, savannah monitors are found to eat baby tortoises, grasshoppers, crickets and their relatives, millipedes, centipedes, caterpillars, snails, beetles, scorpions, frogs, and lizard eggs. Wild specimens will also eat small rodents, baby birds, and small lizards when the opportunity arises.

Remember that if a largely invertebrate-based diet is used, greater care is usually necessary to ensure proper and adequate intake of essential vitamins and minerals. This is much less of a problem when using a largely rodent-based diet.

Prekilled prey can and should be offered to savannah monitors (except do not prekill most insects and "night crawlers," and it is unnecessary for "pinkies" and "fuzzies"). This minimizes the suffering of the prey animal and eliminates the possibility of your monitor suffering a nasty bite by the prey. I have seen some rather severe damage inflicted by rodents, and this can be easily avoided by using dead ones. Also, prekilled animals can be easily placed within the cage or removed if not eaten. There are several ways to kill small rodents. Perhaps the most humane way is to break the animals neck by either grabbing the tail and swiftly striking the back of the head against the edge of a table or holding the animal using a wood dowel firmly behind the head where it meets the neck and firmly pulling the tail (this is especially effective for mice, but not recommended for adult rats). A reasonable method for mass euthanasia, is to place the rodents in a container that can be sealed with a piece of dry ice for about 15 minutes (actually the use of nitrogen gas is perhaps the most humane method).

Caution: Nitrogen gas is an asphyxiation hazard.

It has been suggested that prey items should be offered soon after their removal from the rearing cages. Apparently, the residual food in the prey animal's digestive tract will help supply the monitor with vitamins (especially vitamin C [ascorbic acid and all other compounds that exhibit biological activity similar to ascorbic acid]) and the like. Vitamin C from such "gut contents" has been suggested as having some efficacy in preventing stomatitis (mouth rot) and maintaining the integrity of the skin (Frye 1991, 1995).

Feeding Schedules and Regimens

If all other conditions are adequate, the growth of your savannah monitor will be directly related to its feeding regimen. The growth rate for a savannah monitor will be greatest during the first 2 to 3 years, with much occurring during the first year and a half. When sexual maturity occurs in savannah monitors is difficult to say, but it may occur in *V. olivaceus* at about the end of their second year or the beginning of their third year (apparently similarly for *V. bengalensis*) (Auffenberg 1988, 1994). Both of the above species are approximately the same size as a savannah monitor or a bit larger. When growth slows down, it is best to reduce the feeding regimen. Remember that if you are fortunate enough to get your monitors to breed, or if you buy a gravid female, the feeding schedule should be increased to assure that egg-laying females maintain adequate weight.

Hatchlings up to about 1 ft [33 cm] (TL): Feed monitors this size one to four small (pinkie or fuzzy to young adult) mice every 2 to 3 days. Adjust the size of rodents as the animal grows larger. One can also occasionally offer them 1 1/2 to 4 tablespoons of canned cat food once or twice per month (this seems small, but it is a richer diet). King mealworms, crickets, other insects and arthropods, and earthworms should also be offered (to ensure proper nutrition). Crickets can be utilized as a means to "exercise" young monitors, and it can be quite an amusing spectacle to watch them chasing crickets all about their cages.

One foot [33 cm] to adult size (approx. 3 ft [1 m] or greater, TL): Feed animals of this size one to four adult mice twice a week. As above, insects and other arthropods, earthworms, and even snails should be offered as well. One-footers can be given one-half to three-quarters of a can of canned cat food per month, but do not overdo it. Rodents and/or invertebrates

will provide the best diet, but canned cat food will prove useful for convalescing lizards and when your rodent or invertebrate supplier is temporarily out of stock. Adjust the diet if animals appear overweight or too thin. Of course, as mentioned above, invertebrate-based diets can be used so long as consideration is given to ensure proper nutrition (as previously described).

Adults (3 ft or more, TL): Feed lizards of this age twice a week and adjust to prevent obesity. Some large savannah monitors can be real gluttons and eat as much as 10 or more adult mice per week. Larger savannah monitors can also be offered small weaned rats. If savannah monitors are not given the opportunity to exercise, they will get quite fat, so be careful not to overfeed (be sure also to present opportunities for proper amounts of exercise). If your lizard looks in good health and is not getting too fat or, more rarely, too thin, your regimen is probably adequate. Again, as mentioned above, invertebrate-based diets can be used so long as consideration is given to ensure proper nutrition (as previously described). Some experimentation is recommended here and at the other ages as well, based on type of food, ambient temperature, and amount of activity. Use your good judgment based on the above guidelines, at all times. Keeping records of how much and when you fed, and how the animal responded, can be useful and handy references, especially if you plan to raise more young savannah monitors later.

Stunting

If your monitor is only infrequently fed or offered small amounts of food during its first year or so, it can become stunted. Monitors have high metabolisms for reptiles, and maintaining animals on minimal diets may have serious consequences. It may take much longer to raise an animal to maturity, and it may very likely never reach its full potential size. Be responsible! If you are not willing to adequately feed and house a savannah monitor, do not buy one. A reptile which requires less maintenance, such as many of the species of snakes, may be better suited to your lifestyle.

The Proper Method for Feeding a Monitor

When under 1 ft [33 cm] TL, monitors can be fed without any particular heed to special precautions against personal injury, other than some care when placing or removing the food. But once a larger size is achieved, a herpetoculturist will need to practice safe feeding procedures to avoid injury to himself! What follows are sound feeding practices to avoid the possibility of serious accidental bites.

1. Keep only one lizard per cage. This is a good idea anyway because monitors are known to inflict serious injuries on each other during a fight, and the potential for aggression is fairly high, especially, though not exclusively, among same-sex individuals. They can also injure each other during a "feeding frenzy."

2. Have the food within your easy reach (in case you need to remove it) and be sure you know where the monitor is prior to opening the door of the cage. Obviously, the lizard should not be near the door. If it is near the door, open the door and use a snake stick or blunt broom handle to encourage the lizard to move away. Then, using a pair of long forceps or tongs, introduce the food to some area at a reasonably good distance from the door. NEVER HOLD OR DANGLE THE FOOD ITEM IN YOUR BARE HAND OR ENCOURAGE THE MONITOR TO GRAB THE FOOD FROM YOUR UNPROTECTED HAND! Fingers and hands will become amazingly "prey-like" under such circumstances. The resulting injuries could require a trip to the emergency clinic!

3. If the lizard fails to eat the food (within 12 hours, usually), and it needs to be removed, encourage the monitor to leave the food site, and push or pull the food toward the door of the cage with tongs or long forceps. You can use your hand only if the lizard is nowhere near the food, but the use of tongs or forceps at all times is preferred. Remember, monitor lizards can move incredibly fast when they desire to do so. It is a good idea to put a board or some other shield between you and the lizard when removing food. A good shield can be made by attaching a handle to a section of Plexiglas (size will depend on the dimensions of the cage) so you can see the lizard at all times.

Water

While savannah monitors hail from somewhat arid climates, they still require water, and they drink regularly. Other monitor species may actually spend some time swimming in water (e.g., *V. niloticus*, *V. salvator*, *V. dumerilii*, and *V. indicus*). Captive monitors should regularly have access to a heavy, large container of water. However, care must be taken not to over humidify, especially do not allow the cage to become completely and continuously wet. Most monitors, including many savannah monitors, will enjoy a good soak on occasion. Soaking in warm water will also encourage monitors to defecate (which is a good thing to remember if the lizard becomes constipated). Remember never to allow feces-contaminated water to sit for extended periods, because disease-causing microbes could multiply there. Disinfect and thoroughly rinse any such water container prior to restoring it. In addition to maintaining a clean water container, never allow savannah monitors to remain in soggy cages for extended periods of time and make sure there is adequate ventilation in the enclosure.

Housing and General Maintenance

Enclosures

There are several things to consider before selecting a cage or enclosure for your savannah monitor. Because savannah monitors can grow quite rapidly in their initial year or two of life, it is important not to obtain an enclosure that may eventually become too small. For young specimens, all glass tanks with a locking screen top are available in many pet stores and can be a reasonably good choice. These are easy to find, easy to clean, and provide a good view of your lizard. Purchase one as large as possible because your monitor will definitely grow "into it" (or, perhaps, "out of it" is more accurate). Certainly, a 30- or 55-gallon (113.6 or 208.2 liter) tank would not be too small to start. If you truly wish to be economical, then purchase as large a tank as you can; the space will eventually not go to waste. If you are planning to raise other young specimens in the future, then it might be wise to obtain several different-sized tanks to cycle through the various-sized monitors and economize a bit on space. Certainly, "common sense" should prevail. When your savannah monitor reaches a length of about 3 ft (1 m), it will probably be necessary to get a larger enclosure than most glass tanks could easily provide. There are several choices to be had. One choice is to have a large cage custom built. There are also now a number of high-quality enclosure manufacturers that specialize in reptile housing. Local reptile stores can be a good sources for these cages. One can also find enclosure manufacturers in the advertising section of various herpetological publications.

Finally, one enclosure I have used successfully over the years for very large, tame monitors is the largest of the "take-apart," indoor, galvanized-steel, dog kennels having three sides covered with a plastic painter's tarp (to reduce drafts and defecation splatters). When buying these indoor kennels, the major "trick" is to obtain one with very small space between the bars, so your monitor cannot escape (on occasion, it may be helpful to attach Plexiglas walls along the lower edge of some of these cages). If it can get its head through the bars, normally the rest of the body can follow (or it may get dangerously stuck). Useful ones can be found in many of the larger general-purpose pet stores.

"Minimal enclosures" are not recommended, and any monitor lizard housed under such conditions may exhibit stress, become aggressive, and will certainly not breed. Having said that, a minimum cage size for a monitor should be one and a half to two or more times the snout to vent length (SVL) of the lizard; two-thirds to one times the length of the animal in width; and one to one and half times the length of the animal in height (with height, be sure the lizard cannot peer over the top). Again, the larger the enclosure you can provide, the better the animal will acclimate. Large space is also essential to encourage breeding (Burghardt and Milostan 1995) as well as good physical and mental health for the lizard. Homemade cages can be constructed of wood, with a built-in glass front (or Plexiglas although this can scratch more easily). The top should have screening to provide ventilation and to allow for placement of various lights. Screen sides are not recommended. The type of screen used must be resistant to monitor claws and must be attached very securely to the cage. Plastic-coated welded wire is likely to be the best if screening is used for the sides. The door(s) can be in the front, sides, or top. I prefer to reach down to pick up a monitor (so long as the cage is not more than 3 ft high) rather than coming toward it from the front, especially with frightened or aggressive specimens. Bayless (pers. comm.) notes, however, that reaching down to get the lizard may resemble a bird of prey swooping down to seize it. Hinged, locking doors are preferred to doors that slide up (the potential to "guillotine" must be considered), but doors that slide to one side are usable though not preferred to the hinged type. Probably the best solution for caging the larger species of monitors is to provide them with small rooms or room-sized enclosures with some sort of drainage in the floor for easy cleaning (see Sprackland [1992], Card [1994a, 1995c], Burghardt and Milostan [1995], and Perry-Richardson and Ivanyi [1995] for other housing suggestions and considerations).

The construction of very large "naturalistic" enclosures is beyond the scope and, more than likely, beyond the means of most of the users of this book. Some recent studies deliberate on the "need" for such enclosures by captive herps (but see: Burghardt and Layne 1995; Chiszar et al. 1995; Greenberg 1995; Warwick 1995; Warwick and Steedman 1995) though certainly more information has been published about their use for captive mammal and bird species (see, for example, Gibbons et al. [1994]). Until more research is published that clearly establishes the "need" for such enclosures by amateur herpetoculturists, one can assume that "simpler" constructs which are easy to keep clean, such as those described below, should probably be sufficient for the normal captive maintenance for reptiles (see Cooper and Williams [1995] for the importance of easily cleaned enclosures).

Savannah monitors have surprising strength at any size, and really big ones can seem almost Herculean at times, so all screening must be firmly secured to the top and must be resistant to shredding by their claws. All Plexiglas or glass must be secure and thick enough to be shatterproof. The doors of cages will need to be secured with some kind of locking mechanism. Savannah monitors can be amazingly "clever" and they have good memories when they discover an escape route. So, should a savannah monitor somehow manage to escape from its enclosure, an escape-proof, locked room will provide added security. The additional security of a locked room will mean that your neighbors will not receive unwanted visits from your pet, if it somehow escapes from its enclosure. Should the "unexpected" occur, try to find out how it is escaping, or you will be continually confronted with a lizard on the loose!

Number of Monitors Per Cage

It is usually not a good idea to house more than one monitor per cage for extended lengths of time (Barten 1996; Burghardt and Milostan 1995; Card 1995c; McKeown 1996; Balsai, pers. observ.; but see Burghardt and Layne [1995] for comments concerning the rearing of very young juveniles). This prevents them from doing sudden and serious damage to one another. Monitors are normally solitary animals and should be respected as such. Only when trying to breed them should they be housed together and even then for only as long as is necessary to achieve successful mating (Card 1994a, 1995c; Honegger 1975). Long-term captives can suddenly turn on one another, so just because they do not seem to be aggressive toward each other for the present, does not mean a nasty fight will not occur later. Be alert to the potential for the captive monitor to react aggressively to its reflection (Perry-Richardson and Ivanyi 1995). In addition, animals lower on the "pecking" hierarchy will usually develop "psychologically" related stress disorders (see Gillingham [1995] for a discussion of "normal" reptilian behav-

▲ *A well designed indoor savannah monitor enclosure with a shelter, heat source, and water dish.* Photo by Glen Carlzen.

iors). Finally, it is possible that constant exposure to males may actually suppress the reproductive cycling of females, particularly young females. Alberts (1994b) notes that research is being conducted at the Center for Reproduction of Endangered Species at the San Diego Wild Animal Park into this question of the effects of the "social environment" on first reproduction in white-throated savannah monitors.

Cage Location, Substrates, and Cleaning

It is not normally a good idea to allow monitors to roam free in the house. These lizards are quite inquisitive and have no conception of "fragile," "breakable," "valuable," etc. They will climb upon anything, knock down anything, shred anything, defecate upon anything, randomly pull plugs from sockets, and so forth. A loose monitor in the house is like having an unrestrained mini-Godzilla, and the mentality is not too dissimilar, either. In addition, they also run a risk of injury (see Barten and Bennett

▲ *In warmer areas like southern California, several species of monitors can be housed in outdoor enclosures with heated shelters. Monitors from desert or semi-arid habitats are the best choice for areas with low relative humidity. These setups were designed for keeping and breeding argus monitors. Photo by Chris Estep.*

[1996] for an example of injury sustained by free-roaming monitor) from falls, from falling objects they may have displaced, from electric sockets, etc.

Savannah monitors grow rather large so a reasonably sized room with adequate open space to allow easy maintenance and handling of the animal will be required. An adult savannah monitor in a cluttered room can cause the inadvertent toppling of furniture while being handled. These lizards do not hesitate to flail and will also grab anything within reach. Extracting your lizard from a prize piece of clothing or the drapery can be no small feat. The room should be kept locked when you are not inside, and the lock should be tamper-proof, both against inside and outside residents. The door should always be kept closed. Inspect the room and patch all holes to ensure that any savannah monitor that escapes its enclosure (which normally should not occur, if the cage is properly made and kept locked) will be unable to leave the room. Monitors are notorious escape artists and can squeeze into and under amazingly small openings (Balsai, pers. observ.) or if large and powerful enough, can enlarge a smaller opening (Balsai, pers. observ.). It is common for these lizards to get into the walls via some overlooked opening or hole. Coaxing them out of such a place can be extremely trying and difficult. A savannah monitor which escapes to the outside will surely get you and itself into plenty of trouble! Don't let it happen.

Providing your monitor with a fancy decorated cage would almost certainly require a room-sized enclosure. Most individual herpetoculturists opt not to do this. Simple, and easily maintained conditions will need to be the norm for these lizards, especially the adults. Plants as decorations will be pretty much impossible unless one has the space and conditions to maintain shrubs and trees (Card 1995c; Balsai, pers. observ.). However, some savannah monitors enjoy a good climb, so it is a good idea to provide some sort of climbing branch or pole.

Ground Media

Ideal ground media for maintaining large monitors are newspaper or brown butcher's paper. There have been claims that the ink on newspaper may be detrimental to the health of reptiles, but I am un-aware of any studies that actually help to establish this claim. Many have used this substrate with no problems, often for many years (Balsai, pers. observ.) Both newspaper and brown butcher's paper are inexpensive, easy to obtain and replace, and make cleaning the cage very economical and simple. Many monitors seem to enjoy remodeling the paper to form what appear to be burrows and nests and this activity helps keep their claws shorter (Balsai, pers. observ.). Some herpetoculturists like to use some type of wood chips or bark, (but DO NOT USE CEDAR which can be toxic) or pine shavings as a substrate. Others will use a fine to medium pea gravel. This is acceptable, but beware of the lizard accidentally ingesting any of this material when it feeds because this can cause serious problems (McKeown 1996; McKeown prefers "good quality topsoil" for many reptile species [p. 14]). Unfortunately, many lizards will often pile these loose substrates in one area of the cage. Some herpetoculturists may opt to use an "Astroturf®" or similar artificial grass mat (such as indoor-outdoor carpeting). These latter options may be more aesthetic, but the owner must always remember that savannah monitors (as well as all other monitor species) defecate frequently and in often incredibly large amounts (Card 1995; Balsai, pers. observ.). Additionally, their stools often contain much wet and semi-solid material and typically have a very unpleasant odor. Unless one has a monitor which regularly defecates in a large water container when placed in the cage (a common pattern), one should select easily replaceable ground media. A problem with indoor-outdoor carpeting is that fibers may become wrapped tightly around the digits of the lizard cutting off their circulation here (Strimple 1996). Another ground medium which has been used successfully, particularly with younger savannah monitors, are rabbit or alfalfa pellets, and they may even be digestible if accidently ingested (Barten 1996), but these have some of the same problems that other loose substrates have and may sometimes provide a growth medium for undesirable fungi (Bayless, pers. comm.). Corn-cob substrates are definitely to be avoided as they have caused the deaths of at least two captive savannah monitors via gastrointestinal impaction (McKeown 1996; Bayless, pers. comm.). Sprackland (1992) recommends a "bare floor" which is easily cleaned and cannot be "rear-

▲ *White throated monitors* (Varanus albigularis) *are good choices for keeping in outdoor enclosures where weather permits. Shelters and climbing areas should be provided.* Photo by Chris Estep.

ranged" by the lizard. It is imperative to ensure that such floors are waterproof and claw resistant when the enclosure is homemade.

Shelters

Savannah monitors prefer to have some sort of shelter, especially when they are young (Burghardt and Milostan 1995; Balsai, pers. observ.). Some, instead of using shelters, will bury themselves under the substrate. As a general rule, a monitor will usually acclimate better if provided with a place where it can feel safe and secure (Barten 1996). Easily

47

obtainable and inexpensive shelters can be made from inverted cardboard boxes with a hole cut in the front. Remove these as they become dirty or damaged. More permanent and aesthetic shelters can often be purchased; such as bark, cork sections, or the plastic or ceramic shelters now offered by many reptile stores. The latter are especially useful because they can be easily cleaned. For larger specimens, use specially built, large, wooden shelters or the bigger enclosed cat litter boxes. Shelters can play a significant role in reducing captive stress, yet they are an often overlooked aspect of vivarium design.

Temperature

Monitor lizards are all Old World reptiles which come largely from tropical and subtropical areas. Savannah monitors come from a habitat that is, normally, very hot and rather dry in the day, to somewhat warm, albeit cooler, at night. Their ranges include most of the semi-desert and savannah regions of sub-Saharan Africa. This climate has a modicum of seasonal rainfall, at least in some places, and in the far south can be downright cold at times. Savannah monitors that live where it can get cool may have a short seasonal hibernation period (Cissé 1971; Branch 1988).

With the above in mind, one should provide a daytime temperature of 85 to 90°F (29 to 32°C). At night, the temperature can safely be allowed to drop about 10 to 15°F (to about 68 to 70°F [20 to 21.1°C]). Additionally, at night, one could place a thermostatically controlled heating pad or, even better, a red-bulb heat lamp or ceramic heater (e.g., those marketed by Ram Network or Zoo Med, both in California) to provide a nocturnally accessible warm area.

Keep track of the temperature in your monitor's enclosure room. At the very least, use a high/low thermometer that will indicate the maximum and minimum temperatures for each day. These thermometers are usually manually reset on a daily basis. One of the most recommended types of thermometers is the electronic digital thermometer with an alarm, a sensor (when temperature is too high or too low), and a program for giving daily high/low temperature readings. With one setting, you can obtain a continuous readout of the room's temperature. By switching the setting, you can get a readout for a sensor placed in the basking area or some other desired spot. Knowing what the daily temperature fluctuations are will be helpful in monitoring your lizard's daily health. Always avoid placing the cage in a draft. See Regal (1980), Greek (1991), Avery (1994), Arena and Warwick (1995), and Guillette et al. (1995) for general considerations with respect to the effects of temperature on captive reptiles. Bear in mind that the most desirable temperature setup is one that provides a thermal gradient across a wide range of desirable temperatures through which the lizard can move back and forth, as it behaviorally thermoregulates (much as they do in the wild).

Heating Systems and Methods

Space heaters or room heaters. A somewhat economical method of keeping a room warm is to use an electrical heater, such as a space heater, an electric radiator, or a ceramic electric heater. These work well for keeping animals which have similar temperature requirements. The use of these devices can cause problems, however. The major problem is overheating. The utilization of a backup thermostat on the heater, coupled to an alarm on your thermometer (as described above) can usually go a long way toward preventing this problem, so long as you ensure that both systems are working. Always buy space heaters with safety features to reduce the risk of fire. Additionally, placement can be a problem. If the heater is in a spot where there is a cool draft, it may misread local coolness for the average room temperature and thereby, overheat the room. Temperature gradients will also form in the room. Thus, it will be warmer near the ceiling than on the floor. This must be remembered when placing cages in the room at differing heights and may be somewhat alleviated with the use of ceiling fans, or some similar arrangement. Also, beware of potential fire hazard when placing your space heater. It should be in an open area, away from furniture, curtains or other flammable products. It should also be shielded from any contact by the animal itself. Keep abreast of heater placement, thermostats, and thermometers, and you should be able to avoid tragedy.

Hot rocks. These can be moderately useful as a heat source, especially for small or juvenile monitors, but they should be carefully watched for overheating. Some, especially older models, can also produce hot spots, areas where they are much hotter than at any other site on their surfaces. Subtle thermal burns on the ventral (belly) skin can result when lizards bask on overheating (temperatures of 105°F [40.6°C] or greater) hot rocks. Sprackland (1992) notes that thermoregulation is controlled in many lizards by hormonal signals produced by the pineal eye in response to light (monitors have no externally visible pineal eye, and this may make the above less pertinent to monitors). Such lizards sitting on hot rocks, heating pads, and such, absorbing heat through their bellies, may be unable to produce an early cue to move, resulting in heat damage (burns). Whatever physiological system monitors use to control their body temperatures, sitting upon hot rocks and similar devices is really not what they normally do in the wild. There could be some interaction between cues from the sun and cues from the heated ground that may be lacking when hot rocks and such are used. (However, this does not explain why many reptiles enjoy lying on warm tarmac roads at night, much to their detriment.) It is important to remember these potential physiological responses, no matter what devices are used for providing heat via absorption through the belly. Frequent monitoring of the hot rock should help prevent any problem. The surface temperature of the hot rock should be no hotter than about 85 to 95°F (29 to 35°C). If the rock feels very hot to you, it is too hot. It should feel comfortably warm to your touch (try leaning on it to ensure comfort). Placing a flat rock on top of the hot rock will often diffuse the heat down to a satisfactory level. A significantly better idea is to control the hot rock with a dimmer switch. As your monitor grows larger, you will have to consider an alternative source of heat. There can be some confusion as to how hot rocks should be used. Some are actually designed to be buried under substrate whereas others are not. Note, that hot rocks and similar devices are not meant to heat an entire cage and were never designed to do so. They should never serve as the sole source of heat for monitor lizards or any other reptile. Many authors (e.g., McKeown 1996) do not recommend their use and there are certainly better sources of heat for these lizards.

Incandescent lights and ceramic heaters. Incandescent floodlights or spotlights (75 watts and higher depending on the temperature) can be used to keep a savannah monitor warm. Just remember to use a thermometer to assure that the basking site is within the desirable range (85 to 95°F [29 to 35°C]). In large, tall enclosures, infrared bulbs (like the GE infrared reflector 115–125 V/250-watt type, that are used in fast-food restaurants to keep French fries warm) are particularly recommended because they can be kept on at night, if necessary, without any detriment to the animal (i.e., it is not in perpetual daylight). Whatever type of bulb you decide on, ensure that the fixture and the bulb do not directly contact the animal in any way. Reptiles are not normally exposed to heat of such potentially damaging temperatures in the wild and often do not seem to notice burn injuries as they are occurring. The resulting burns can be very traumatic and even fatal (see figure 2-8 of a savannah monitor in McKeown [1996]). After the bulb has been on about an hour, measure the temperature of the basking area directly under the bulb and to some distance out to ensure this area is not too hot. Again, as with space heaters, make sure that nothing flammable can contact or be ignited by the bulb, to avoid a fire. An interesting and somewhat elaborate setup using incandescent lamps and thermostats was described by Freer (1993) for use with his Dumeril's monitor. Bayless (pers. comm.) indicated that red incandescent lights seem to cause lethargy in at least some lizards. The newer ceramic heaters (e.g., those marketed by Ram Network or Zoo Med, both in California) are designed to fit into light sockets and may actually be even better than incandescent bulb heaters because they do not necessarily emit potentially unwanted light with the heat.

Heating pads. Subtank reptile and standard heating pads can be useful for providing heat to savannah monitors though they may be too small for some larger species or specimens. Be sure that the surfaces of any heating pads cannot be, or do not become damaged by the lizard's claws (the vast majority are probably best used under the tank). Ensure that these devices are waterproof before placing into a tank. Again these should not be the sole source of heat and are not the most desirable.

Fiberglass heating pads or pig blankets. These devices are sold in feed stores and some specialized reptile stores. Some herpetoculturists claim that these are among the best heating units for large reptiles. Basically, they are moderately large (at least 3 ft ∞ 1 ft [1 m ∞ 0.31 m]), ridged, fiberglass, enclosed units that provide high surface heat over a broad area. When used with the thermostat that can be special ordered from the manufacturer, these may be ideal for savannah monitors and, of course, other large monitor species. Exercise some caution because these devices can have some of the "disadvantages" of hot rocks if used improperly.

Lighting

Most animals require circadian (24-hour) light/dark cycles, and savannah monitors are no exception. Provide monitors with 12 to 14 hours of daylight, using when possible, a combination of artificial and natural light. The days are longer in Africa in the summer and shorter in winter (Bayless, pers. comm.). Many herpetoculturists will use a Vita-Lite® or some similar full-spectrum light for their animals. I have also used regular fluorescent bulbs with, seemingly, as much success (see also Gehrmann et al. 1991). It is possible, though, that subtle benefits can be derived from lights that simulate natural daylight, so the use of full-spectrum bulbs should definitely be considered (especially for animals that the herpetoculturist wishes to mate). Unlike some monitor keepers, I do not advocate the use of any black or ultraviolet light as the potential for harm (especially to the eyes [e.g., blindness] and skin; see Ross and Marzec 1990), via excess or misuse, may exceed any benefit (see also Perry-Richardson and Ivanyi [1995] and Gehrmann [1987, 1994a,b, 1996] for information about the use of ultraviolet lights). With proper diet, possibly including some modicum of supplementation, your monitor should not require an ultraviolet light (but see Alberts [1994a] for more on this topic) to synthesize vitamin D_3 (cholecalciferol). If the design of your vivarium allows it (some herpetoculturists have specially designed accesses to outdoor vivaria), provide regular access to natural, unfiltered sunlight though this is not necessarily required for the maintenance of monitors in captivity. See Regal (1980), Gehrmann (1987, 1994a,b, 1996), and Arena and Warwick (1995) for general considerations with respect to the effects of light requirements on captive reptiles.

Maintenance

The living quarters of your savannah monitor will need regular hygienic maintenance (for general method and information, see Wright 1993c). Remove feces and other waste products as well as any soiled substrate. Clean the cage with some sort of mild disinfectant, at least once a week. I prefer (see also Barten 1996) either a dilute solution of Nolvasan-S® (chlorihexidine) or dilute (to between 5 and 15% [Barten (1996) uses 3%]) sodium hypochlorite bleach (common household bleach solution such as Clorox® though be aware that bleach may cause skin problems for certain species such as mangrove monitors). Another possibility is Roccal-D at between 1:200 (small cages) and 1:400 (large cages) (McKeown 1996). NEVER USE PHENOLIC COMPOUNDS, SUCH AS LYSOL®, BECAUSE THEIR RESIDUES COULD BE TOXIC! Be sure to remove all traces of disinfectant. The water container should be washed, disinfected, thoroughly rinsed, and refilled with fresh water when ever necessary. If the water vessel is large enough, monitors may climb into it and soak. In the process, many lizards will defecate, so remove such soiled water as soon as possible, disinfect the container, and replace the water. If the monitor is housed in large quarters (especially room sized), it would probably be very convenient to install a drain to allow for frequent hosing down and washing away of the waste. See Chiszar et al. (1995) for some interesting considerations concerning the behavioral reactions of herps to manipulations relating to routine husbandry, especially with respect to artificial and natural chemical cues (particularly as applied to cage cleaning).

Equipment

A very useful piece of equipment for dealing with large monitors is a pair of thick, long-cuffed, leather gloves, such as those used by welders or hedge-cutters. Another tool I have used on occasion is a broom handle. Sometimes moderately large monitors

◄ *A leucistic Nile monitor* (Varanus niloticus). *Photo by Chris Estep.*

can be induced to cling to the broom handle and thereby, with modest restraint, be moved about. I have used this technique with some success largely with moderately difficult lizards, especially the arboreal species, but some savannah monitors can be "taught" this trick. A modest-sized, fairly heavy snake hook turned sideways can also serve as well. Some suggestions given by Wise (1994) for crocodilians (see also Barten 1996) can be easily modified for use with large monitor lizards. Wise's method of using a sponge mop to assist in pinning an animal for grasping is especially promising. Remember too, that with a modicum of care, monitors can, if necessary, be lifted by the tail (near the hips) for very short periods and distances. This works especially well with smaller animals, without risk of breaking the tail because these lizards do not have caudal autotomy (the self-fracturing tail possessed by most lizard families). Avoid doing this with really "squirmy" or aggressive animals and in all cases where the animal is handled by the tail, be sure to grasp the tail fairly close to the hips. Goggles may be another useful item, particularly to protect the handler's eyes from accidental or intentional tail lashes to the eyes. *Varanus albigularis* will apparently "aim" for the eyes of its captors (Bayless, pers. comm.).

Grooming and Handling

Although it is not possible to "groom" a savannah monitor in the sense of a dog or cat, certain things can be done to facilitate handling and benefit the health of your lizard.

1. Claw trimming

Because many setups for your monitor may not provide a surface that is rough enough or a space large enough to allow your lizard to wear down its claws, regular trimming of the claws will probably be necessary. Monitors will naturally develop very sharp, pointed claws that can inflict such a significant amount of superficial damage to your skin that handling them without some protection can result in multiple small puncture wounds, deep scratches, and excruciating pain. If the claws are kept trimmed, your monitor can be handled without damage to yourself or your clothes.

Trimming the claws of adult monitors will require two (or even better, three) people and good illumination. The person handling the lizard should hold it with both hands (wear gloves). One hand should encircle the neck and area above the forelegs. The other hand should encircle the area above the hind legs. With every large animal, one person should hold onto the front end and the other onto the hip area. The tail should be stabilized against one's body or a firm flat surface. Remember that monitors will whip and thrash their tails. Hold the monitor firmly and tilt it vertically or sideways, so that the lizard's "belly" is toward the person trimming the claws. Beware, some monitors will also take this opportunity to defecate on you!

Trim the claws as per the following procedure:

a. Use rubbing alcohol or Betadine® and apply via a cotton swab or gauze pad to the claws and the surrounding areas of the "hand" or foot to be trimmed. This will disinfect this area.

b. Hold the lizard's finger or toe at the base of the claw and examine carefully under a good light. Clip the point where you can see no blood vessels or anything else. In other words, you should be able to see (more or less) clear through the claw without encountering any other tissues. Use nail clippers or dog/cat nail clippers to cut the point and then file any sharp edges with a nail file or emery board. Be very meticulous because sometimes the claws can be very dark (especially in large animals), and blood vessels can be very hard to see. When in doubt, cut only the sharp tip. If you accidentally "nick" any blood vessels or other nail tissues and the lizard bleeds, wipe the claw with some disinfectant and dip the bleeding tip into cornstarch or KwikStop® (be sure to have these ready just in case). An alternative to doing this yourself is to hire the services of skilled personnel of pet shops (if they are willing) that deal heavily in birds. They trim bird claws regularly, and the process is quite similar. Some veterinarians are probably capable of providing this service as well. Remember, clip only the pointed tip, as cutting the claw's base can result in much more serious bleeding, and the risk of infection is increased. With some practice, anyone can become reasonably good at performing this occasional but necessary task.

2. General grooming

Keeping your monitor clean is essential for its long-term good health. Many savannah monitors enjoy a good "soak," so it is appropriate to offer the lizard a large container of warm water at least every couple of weeks. Large plastic tubs or large cat litter boxes are very useful for this purpose. For very large animals, some type of self-draining tub would be very useful. The temperature of the water should be warm but not hot to the touch. Be sure that the water level barely covers the back of the animal and check on the lizard frequently. After soaking, you can frequently remove any loose skin still clinging to your savannah monitor. Be sure to adequately dry off your monitor to prevent any sudden chill, and thereby, the risk of respiratory ailments. As a general rule, the use of bathtubs is not recommended for this purpose. Large tubs in a securely locked enclosure are preferable because this method will prevent any risk of escape. Sanitation should be another consideration for avoiding the use of bathtubs.

▲ *Careful initial selection of a monitor and regular handling will be necessary to develop a good pet-owner relationship. Juvenile monitors are often initially flighty but many settle down as they get older. Nile monitors can vary greatly in personality and selection of a calm animal can be critical with this species.* Photo by Chris Estep.

Some people use a an "old" toothbrush and gently rub the dorsum, legs, etc. Some individuals seem to "enjoy" this (Bayless, pers. comm.) whereas others do not and may even become irritated and aggressive after a short period of this activity (Balsai, pers. observ.). This method is useful in that it does not tear loose skin off prematurely.

3. Grasping and general handling

Monitors, especially large, untamed, wild-caught animals, require some care when grasped and during handling. If the animal is enraged or in some way irritated or just normally has a ferocious temper, it may be quite difficult to grab hold. In many zoos, large fierce monitors are lassoed when necessary, similar to the method described by Wise (1994) for crocodilians. If approach becomes difficult, indi-vidual handlers could drop a cloth over the head of the lizard to obscure its vision and ease the capture (Card 1995c; Barten 1996; Balsai, pers. observ.). Many monitors can even be wrapped in towels or some other strong cloth as an aid to restraint (Barten 1996). Ferocious animals may even require several handlers

for restraint. It is necessary to secure the head of such animals and I find this is best achieved by firmly gripping the lizard behind the head, much like one would do with a snake (Card 1995c). Holding the animal about the neck may be required, but care must obviously be taken to avoid strangling the animal. The pelvic area can be grasped so that the thumb and index finger of the other hand is placed around the hips and one rear limb can be allowed to protrude from between the middle and ring fingers (Card 1995c). The tail must be controlled either by holding firmly under the arm pit or better yet, by an assistant (Card 1995c). Keep the claws blunt so that they cannot also be used to inflict damage during handling. Tamer animals can be held with one hand controlling the head and front end while the body is supported with one arm (hand about the pelvic area) and the lizard's body braced against the body of the restrainer (tail might be held under the arm as described above). Occasionally the mouth may need to be taped if the lizard (especially if it is not tame) must be handled for a fairly long period (as de-

▲ *It is important to offer water for bathing at least every couple of weeks. Note, this container is large enough for the animal to drink from and soak its entire body. Photo by Chris Estep.*

61

scribed for crocodilians [Wise 1994]). Be aware that many monitors, particularly when angry or frightened, will expel copious amounts of fecal matter upon the handler, so care must be made to ensure the cloacal area is held away from the body. This feces may even come out with such force as to be almost like a projectile (Card 1995c).

Developing a "Pet/Owner" Relationship

The main point to keep in mind when developing a "pet/owner" relationship with your savannah monitor is to be totally nonthreatening to your lizard. Certainly, this type of relationship can be developed far more easily with captive-raised adults (which were probably already pets) or young animals. When a captive savannah monitor habituates to humans, it will no longer show any desire to run away or attack. This means the animal will be calm when approached and, to some degree, will allow itself to be handled and carried. Such animals will often allow themselves to be petted or otherwise touched. An established monitor will normally approach you when you are bringing it food and will readily accept food offered from forceps. It should be relatively calm when moved about to other parts of your home. Basically, a pet savannah monitor loses its fear of humans and can then be one of the best and most rewarding reptile pets. To achieve this relationship, frequent and regular nonthreatening interaction will be required.

▲ *An angry white-throated monitor (Varanus albigularis) ready to lash out with its tail. Photographed at the Norden Zoo by Mark Bayless.*

After acclimation, you can begin short periods of interaction. Keep any other pets (especially cats and dogs) out of sight and smell of your new lizard during your initial taming and handling sessions as these can frighten your monitor. Bear in mind that savannah monitors will usually not tolerate extended periods of handling or petting, no matter how tame. Never carry your lizard outside or in public places because your monitor may suddenly become frightened, and you may lose it. Also, you do not want to risk frightening the general public and thereby add to the notion that herpetoculturists are irresponsible.

Various herpetoculturists have differing approaches to working with monitors. Prior to and after handling your monitor, be sure that your hands are clean and washed and that you have not recently handled any food for the lizard. You could begin by scratching a monitor behind the head or on the back of its neck, then progress to lightly stroking its sides. You might then slowly pick up the lizard and then place it back in the cage a few times. With small animals, it is a good technique to often take them out of the cage and allow them to travel from one hand to another while trying to persuade them to do so as calmly as possible. Almost certainly, when trying this technique, your lizard will attempt to run away, but if caught and persuaded after several attempts to move slowly from one hand to the next, your savannah monitor will usually calm down and do what you want it to do. This is the initial step in getting your lizard familiar with being picked up and handled. Remember, also, that trimmed claws will make the handling of your lizard easier on you. If you stroke the back of its neck and sides, this can often enhance your lizard's favorable response to your handling. Often, after a period of a few weeks, you will probably notice that your monitor is becoming calmer. Its behavior will guide you in deciding the extent that it can be left out of its cage and in a familiar area. Bear in mind, though, that excessive handling can promote stress-related disorders.

▼ *A tame adult ornate Nile monitor* (Varanus niloticus ornatus). *Photo by Greg Naclerio.*

The degree of tameness you get with your monitor will largely depend on the amount of time and effort you invest in interacting with it. I have seen (and owned) savannah monitors so tame that they would remain quite still and allow many strangers to observe and even touch them. I have had several that were "dog-tame," and one that would allow me to pose it for humorous holiday snapshots (see dedication).

The use of a small dog or cat harness combined with a leash, or better yet, perhaps those specially marketed for use with lizards, might be very useful for preventing a tame savannah monitor from suddenly darting off at a time or place where this would not be convenient. A harness can also be used to train and control your lizard when allowing it to roam about the house. Always be on the alert for escapes or the animal becoming entangled in the leash or harness (which may lead to injury). However, I do not advocate walking the lizard about the neighborhood or even unsupervised harnessing in a back yard.

Savannah Monitor Personalities

If you encounter enough savannah monitors, you will soon discover that they can exhibit a wide variety of "personalities." Some are extroverted and even appear to tolerate the presence of humans quite well. Some will be nervous, shy, and possibly even scared. Some monitors will even be feisty and asocial, lashing their tails and generally acting a bit snappy. Thus, not all savannah monitors will be great pets. Some are, at best, merely tolerant of humans and will only make good display animals. If one animal turns out to not be such a great pet, perhaps you might consider acquiring another (given the space). A couple of savannah monitors are not much more time consuming or difficult to keep than one.

▲ *Mangrove monitor* (Varanus indicus) *performing an aggressive display. These animals are currently being imported in small numbers from the Solomon Islands.*
Photo by Glen Carlzen.

A method for controlling biting was recently reported by Attum (1994). This involves the use of a commercially available fluid called Bitter Apple® (actually a chewing deterrent for dogs) and is marketed by Valhar Chemical Corporation. Attum (1994) used it to control biting by a ferocious tegu and succeeded by spraying this substance on a glove. After biting the glove, the tegu immediately released it. Later, he merely sprayed his hand with this deterrent, and the tegu refused to bite. The entire "training" process took at least a month, however, so do not expect instant fulfillment. Attum reported that the tegu does not even attack his "unscented hand" now! He also successfully used this product with an iguana. I have also had some success using this product with aggressive monitors, but again, it takes some patience and time.

It is important for readers to be able to recognize when a monitor lizard is angry and the stereotypical threat/display behaviors that accompany this reaction. Sometimes an angry monitor will turn toward a person with its mouth wide open. This is normally followed by a sudden lunge if you get too close! At other times the lizard will hiss loudly, inflate its throat, and produce a pronounced curve in the neck by bowing its head (called a raised "roach" [Auffenberg 1978, 1981]). This may be accompanied by rather violent twitching, curling, and possibly lashing of the tail. Sometimes they may slowly sway their bodies. When monitor lizards are angry or afraid, they can be amazingly aggressive, and handling the animal at that time may result in a serious bite. Injuries by large specimens may require stitches. Bites by monitors can be a serious problem and often take relatively long to heal (Balsai, pers. observ.) Many monitors, including savannahs, lash their tails as a threat, and a "smack" by any species can be rather unpleasant. Savannah monitors have very thick tails that actually feel like clubs. Finally, many monitors will readily defecate upon anyone who seizes and handles them when they are afraid. Treat them with respect and enjoy their company.

Savannah monitors and other monitor species tend to undergo developmental changes in personality. Many hatchlings tend to be a bit flighty, nervous, or even aggressive (this is probably "normal" behavior for juvenile monitors). Later, as they mature, a significant percentage will calm down, but some may become even more wary and aggressive.

Interpreting Monitor Lizard Stereotypical Behaviors

As mentioned in the above section, it is a good idea to be able to recognize the so-called "stereotypical" behaviors exhibited by monitor lizards under different conditions. The most important from the standpoint of the herpetoculturist are the threat behaviors.

Threat Behaviors

Most of these behaviors are described above. Some species of monitors (though not savannah monitors), such as the argus, Gould's, and Bengal monitors will also occasionally rear up on their hind legs. This can

be quite amazing to behold and, if the lizard is large, even rather intimidating. These monitors will sporadically do this to take stock of their surroundings, and this posture should not be interpreted as only a result of anger. Angry monitors will often turn to show their broad sides, raise their bodies very high on all four legs (Barten 1996), arch their backs, and puff out the throat while showing a "raised roach" (see above for the meaning of this expression). Nearly all threats are accompanied by loud hissing and puffing. This can be incredibly loud at times! It is not recommended that anyone attempt to handle such annoyed lizards. Ditmars (1933) remarked about how placing monitor lizards in natural sunlight can sometimes cause even the most docile specimens to become suddenly wildly aggressive. I as well as others have subsequently observed this phenomenon.

▲ *"Goliath," a tame savannah monitor resting on top of its cage in an apartment in New York City. Photo by Philippe de Vosjoli.*

Group Behavior

Occasionally, other behaviors may be noted, particularly when these lizards interact with conspecifics. These are usually observed when the lizards are mating or while several individuals are establishing social hierarchies and/or territories. Most of these behaviors involve the animals posturing and assuming various stances with respect to one another. Males of several species (e.g., Asian water monitors, Nile monitors, Timor monitors, savannah monitors, white-throated monitors, and argus/Gould's monitors) will engage in ritualistic combat. Larger species, such as *V. salvadorii*, *V. salvator*, and *V. gouldii*, will even wrestle each other while assuming an upright posture. They grip each other with their forelegs only, and push and shove. Smaller species, such as *V. timorensis*, will wrap about each other with both the forelegs and hind legs, at least initially, and they will roll about while so entwined. During these interactions, the combatants are trying to overpower each other and establish dominance. Sometimes they may inflict damage on each other with the teeth and claws, but usually it is only after dominance is established that the loser may get bitten by the winner. Some species do not normally bite each other (e.g., *V. salvator*) whereas others usually do (e.g., *V. niloticus*) (see Horn et al. 1994).

Hunting Behavior

Those who are familiar with monitors will recognize the typical hunting behaviors of these lizards. The animals will exhibit a somewhat swaying or swinging walk, accompanied by side-to-side motions of the head. These head motions are always accompanied by frequent tongue flicks, that bring particles to the Jacobson's organs on the roof of the mouth. If food is placed in the cage at this time, the lizard will normally quickly locate and seize the food. In addition, observation of your pet monitor will reveal how it shuffles from warm to cool to warm again as it thermoregulates. Detailed descriptions about monitor behavior can be found in Auffenberg (1978, 1981, 1983, 1988, 1994), Daltry (1991), and Green and King (1993).

Breeding Behavior

Breeding behavior in monitors has some characteristic components to it. A male will typically "nuzzle" a female and tongue flick her about the neck. He will also rub his head along her back and will "nuzzle" her cloacal area, before mounting atop her body and thrusting his cloacal area aside hers. The approach is from either side and he uses his tail to raise the female's tail upward. The female will then raise the leg closest to the male to allow copulation to commence. Insertion is initiated by several lateral pelvic movements and then they may lie quietly for a time. Eventually separation will occur, though copulations may take place many times over a period of several days (one pair of lace monitors [*V. varius*] were seen to copulate 16 times in one hour). Eventually males and females lose interest and go their own ways (at least in the wild, so it is good to separate such pairs at this time). In some species the male may bite the female on the neck while upon her back (e.g., Komodo monitors) and some species "immobilize" their mates with a tight foreleg embrace (e.g., Komodo monitors, Gray's monitor). This immobilization seems necessary in species where females are aggressive. In other species, males may rub their heads on the top of the female's head (e.g., Bengal monitors). Pair bonds may be formed of varying duration, and some females may mate with several males in a sort of "mating assemblage" (Green and King 1993; Auffenberg 1978, 1981, 1983, 1988, 1994). Usually, though, the appearance of other males to a mating female will initiate separation and combat behavior between males, examples of which have been described above.

Breeding

Before attempting to captive breed any reptile species, one must consider many different factors: the sexual behavior of the female and male reptiles under study, the possibility that pheromones may be involved, the probability that the reptile species under study responds to various endogenous rhythms (particularly circannual rhythms), the roles of coloration and sexual dimorphism, "energy budgets," territoriality, hibernation, neuroendocrine influences, and environmental influences on both mating behavior and, of course, egg incubation. These subjects are all too involved and complicated to be discussed here, but interested readers are referred to the following references for further insight into these phenomena. The entire reproductive biology section of *Captive Management and Conservation of Amphibians and Reptiles*, edited by James B. Murphy et al. (1994, p. 119–221, as well as Honegger (1975), Murphy and Collins (1980), Duvall et al. (1982), Gregory (1982) Hubert (1985), Saint Girons (1985), Frye (1991), Gans and Crews (1992), Vitt and Pianka (1994), Licht (1995), and DeNardo (1996). Additional useful information can also be gleaned from Burghardt and Layne (1995), Burghardt and Milostan (1995), and Perry-Richardson and Ivanyi (1995).

Captive breeding of monitors has improved somewhat since the last edition of this book. However, repeated and consistent breeding of any species still remains somewhat elusive for most species. Certainly, captive breeding for any species of varanid do not seem to be well publicized, particularly by private individuals. It is important to note that the American Zoo and Aquarium Association (AZA) appears to consider the captive "birth" and breeding of monitor lizards to be an event worth reporting in their publication *Communiqué*. My survey reveals eight published reports (see: Wanner 1991; Pfaff 1992; Ettling 1992; Walsh and Rosscoe 1992; Card 1993; Rish 1994; Conners 1994; Fost 1995) since February 1991 (the time my membership began).

There seems, as yet, to be no formula for the breeding of monitor lizards as there seems to be for the breeding of many other reptiles, and there are several impediments. The small number of breeding records and the generally poor breeding success may, in part, be attributed to minimal efforts by members of the private sector to develop the commercial breeding of monitor lizards. At this point in time, the space, costs, and labor of developing captive breeding of monitor lizards does not appear to be a profitable venture, particularly with the less expensive species now imported in large numbers (such as savannah and Nile monitors). Possibly, better management of wild populations and the development of field culture in the countries of origin are a better course of action with the larger species. Nonetheless, more efforts should be made in this area by hobbyists, particularly with the rarer species, to develop a methodology for sustained multigeneration propagation. The knowledge derived from developing this methodology may prove invaluable in the future conservation of varanid species. If you are keeping one monitor lizard, why don't you consider obtaining a mate for it? In addition, be sure to get the record and method of any successes published. It is also important to note as many conditions that lead to captive breeding success as possible. Remember, those "little" details may end up being the significant determinants to your success, so be sure to keep detailed and careful records.

For those wishing to attempt to breed monitor lizards, the following are guidelines which could contribute to success (remember, there is still as yet, no established breeding formula).

1)   If possible, start with captive-raised animals. The successful adjustment of captive raised monitors to captivity may facilitate their interest in breeding more readily than imported adults (this tends to be true of any reptile). In addition, give the animals as much three-dimensional space as possible. Height may be as important as length and width, and this must certainly be true for those species that are arboreal or partially so (Burghardt and Milostan 1995; Honegger 1975). Further, be sure to have a proper thermal regime, particularly with respect to gradients.

2)   Try to determine the sex of your animals (see Sexing, Growth, and Longevity section in Chapter 1). Without at least one sexual pair, you have, of course, no chance of breeding your animals. If you have the facilities to maintain several pairs, your chances of success will be greatly increased. It is quite likely that some pairs will breed some of the time, and that certain pairs or combinations will be more likely to breed than others. If one pair does not seem interested, try switching partners. In addition, keep all individuals housed separately until breeding is to be attempted (Honegger 1975; Card 1994a, 1995c; Burghardt and Milostan 1995). After the animals show no further interest in breeding, separate them again (Honegger 1975; Card 1994a, 1995c). According to Card (1994a), animals are introduced for mating

▲ *Adult Timor monitor* (Varanus timorensis). *Because of their small size, dwarf monitors are generally better candidates for breeding projects. Photo by Glen Carlzen.*

when the photoperiod begins to lengthen (which in Dallas seems to start in February and does not necessarily coincide with the "natural breeding season"). Be aware of other environmental factors that might also be varied, such as relative humidity, and alter these as well. Attempt experiments where these factors are altered individually and in combination.

3) Your savannah monitors should be sexually mature. Size is also a valid criterion. Both Andrews (1995) and Alberts (1994b) indicated that readiness to breed (in females, anyway) can be related to body length. De Buffrénil et al. (1994) showed that male Nile monitors grow at a faster and steadier rate than females and that males slow down in growth later than females (on average after 9 years vs. 6 years). Savannah monitors 2.5 ft or greater in total length are virtually certain to be sexually mature animals. They should probably be at least 2.5 years (under optimal conditions) and preferably 3 years or more if captive-raised. The growth rate of adult monitors is drasti-

▲ *Immature Dumeril's or brown rough-necked monitor. Overall, this is a docile and easily maintained species. It has recently been successfully bred in captivity. Photo by Glen Carlzen.*

cally reduced compared to that of immature monitors, and reduced growth rate can possibly be used as a criterion for sexual maturity.

4)   The animals should have good weight but should not be grossly obese. A good diet and good health are imperative (DeNardo 1996). This is particularly true for female animals, which need to produce and yolk eggs. It may also be a good idea to integrate the fact that in the wild, many species of monitors are influenced by a seasonal availability of their food. This does influence the breeding of these lizards in nature where egg laying and hatching are coordinated to periods of higher food availability for the neonates.

5)   Create a period of rest/cooling/fasting. As a rule, many reptiles do not breed when environmental conditions remain constant, and this appears to be true with many species of monitors. With savannah monitors, a rest period can be induced in early fall, though some private breeders and the Rotterdam Zoo have successfully induced breeding in white-throated monitors *(V. albigularis)* by cooling them in the winter (see, for example, Visser 1981). Remember, this species of monitor comes from areas of Southern Africa that have a cool period where the temperature significantly drops for a period of time (Branch 1988; Alden et al. 1995). A period of rest/inactivity, usually induced through a period of cooling and fasting that may also include a period of reduced day length, will often alter physiological pathways in reptiles resulting in subsequent reproductive processes and behaviors. A methodology for inducing a rest period in savannah monitors should include:

a) Keep pairs separate.

b) Reduce the temperature range at which the animals are maintained by 10°F (mid to upper 60s to lower 70s [°F] at night and upper 70s to low 80s during the day) for a period of 4 to 6 weeks.

c) During that time, reduce the photoperiod to 10 hours of light versus 14 hours of darkness. This should also result in 14 hours of night cooling.

d) Have the animals fast, or feed them very reduced amounts.

6) After the rest period, reestablish temperatures, preferably in the high range and raise the photoperiod to 14 or more hours of daylight per day (even up to 24 hours for short periods has been recommended by some herpetoculturists to induce breeding), feed heavily, and augment the diet with a vitamin/mineral supplement. During the following weeks, introduce the female into the male's vivarium for one to three days at a time at regular intervals (every week or every 2 weeks). Keep animals under surveillance because some animals may fight, but do not confuse combat with mating behavior (see Bayless 1992a, 1994).

7) Once copulatory attempts cease, the animals should be kept separated. If successful breeding has occurred, egg laying will usually follow 4 to 6 weeks after the observation of copulation. Savannah moni-

tors are known to lay their eggs in termite nests in the wild (Strimple 1988; Bayless 1994), and one captive animal actually laid them in PVC tubing (Bayless and Reynolds 1992). It seems, though, that they will place the eggs down on the substrate when necessary (Bayless and Huffaker 1992). To be sure, though, it is unknown whether the type of substrate has much effect on egg retention by female monitor lizards. Horn in Auffenberg (1994) noted that neonate Bengal monitors have very little yolk left when they hatch. Horn believes this is due to a long incubation period. A potential importance of this for captive monitor lizards (among other things) is that female monitors may retain the eggs longer while searching for a suitable place to lay the eggs. This causes the eggs to acquire a thicker shell than usual and thicker shells require greater movement and strength from these babies when they attempt to hatch. Perhaps this is a reason why some captive-laid eggs fail to hatch.

8)   The eggs, about 1.5 to 1.8 in. (3.7 to 4.5 cm) in length for savannah monitors, can be incubated in moistened vermiculite (Terralite™, grade 3) at the

▲ *This is a young adult Savannah monitor. This species grows rapidly and can be sexually mature by the second year when raised under captive conditions.*

79

proportions of 50% vermiculite and 50% water (by weight) at 85 to 86°F (29 to 30°C) (see Card 1994; Douglas 1994 [1993]; Packard and Phillips 1994). Containers used vary, but large plastic buckets and glass jars are commonly used, as well as small aquaria. What is important is that the container have a lid capable of allowing the humidity of the enclosed air to reach saturation. Card (1994) recommends opening the containers on occasion to allow fresh air to enter. They should hatch in 165 to 195 days though incubation temperature is an important factor when figuring hatching times.

9) Eggs should never be turned (a light pencil mark can be made on the upper surface to help ensure against this). It is presently not known whether incubation temperatures affect the sex of monitor lizards, but indications seem to be that it does not (Wright 1993b; but see Phillips and Packard [1994] for an elaboration about the importance of temperature and humidity for hatchling physical characteristics).

10) It was noted that the tails of all species of monitors are "short" upon hatching (Mertens 1942), but it has been recently noted this is not true in every case (Horn and Visser 1991). Presumably this short tail may allow for full utilization of the space within the egg (Horn and Visser 1991), and, of course, the body length to tail length of these "affected" monitor species does change with growth.

11) Upon hatching, monitors have been noted not to begin feeding immediately (Horn and Visser 1991). For example, in the case of black rough-necked monitors *(V. rudicollis)* and lace monitors *(V. varius)*, the babies do not begin eating until about 8 to 10 days after hatching whereas others, such as the Timor's monitor *(V. timorensis)* and the Cape monitor (Staedeli 1962), will commence feeding after about 1 to 4 days.

Much of the above is a compilation of generalizations that will have to be confirmed and, very likely, drastically modified through "experimentation."

Possibly only a very brief rest period is required. Perhaps environmental changes other than a cool rest period will be the key triggers to successful breeding. There is still plenty of room for original and worthwhile research in this area, and you don't have to be a Ph.D. to accomplish good work as long as you keep careful and meticulous records.

For more information on the breeding of monitor lizards, the following references (see table below), in addition to those cited in the text above, should be very useful. [Note: this list does not claim completeness. Some of the other references in the bibliography have useful breeding information, and additional breeding citations may also be listed in the Notes on Other Monitor Species section.]

General References for Monitors

Horn and Visser 1989;
Sprackland 1991, 1992;
Balsai 1993;
Card 1994a, 1995c

Some Monitor Species Discussed in this Book

Murphy 1971; Thissen 1992 *(V. acanthurus)*
Barker 1984; Card 1994c *(V. prasinus)*
Garrett and Peterson 1991 *(V. beccarii)*
Irwin 1986 [1991]; Card 1994b, 1995a; Limpus 1995 *(V. gouldii)*
Bayless 1994; Roder and Horn 1994 *(V. exanthematicus)*
Radford and Paine 1989 *(V. dumerili)*
Chippindale 1991 *(V. timorensis)*

Endangered Monitor Species

Auffenberg 1978, 1981; Lange 1989; Walsh et al. 1993 *(V. komodoensis)*
Auffenberg 1983, 1994;
Gorman 1993 *(V. bengalensis)*
Visser 1985 [1992] *(V. flavescens)*
Perry et al. 1993 *(V. griseus)*
McCoid and Hensley 1991 *(V. indicus)*

Monitor Species Not Commonly Available

Auffenberg 1988; Card 1995b *(V. olivaceus)*
Boyer and Lamoreaux 1983 *(V. gilleni)*
Bredl and Schwaner 1983; Markwell 1983; Carter 1990; Horn 1991 *(V. varius)*
Eidenmüller 1991, 1992, 1995; Irwin 1986 [1991] *(V. mertensi)*
O'Dell 1992 *(V. tristus)*
Strimple and Strimple 1996 *(V. giganteus)*

A juvenile white throated monitor (Varanus albigularis). *Photo by Paul Freed.*

The Colombian tegu (Tupinambis t. nigropunctatus) *is the tegu species most frequently imported for the pet trade. Photo by David Northcott, Nature's Lens.*

Dumeril's monitor (Varanus dumerilii). *Photo by Bill Love, Blue Chameleon Ventures.*

A hatchling Dumeril's monitor. Photo by Bill Love, Blue Chameleon Ventures.

A mangrove monitor (Varanus indicus). Photo by Paul Freed.

A Nile monitor (Varanus niloticus). Photo by David Northcott, Nature's Lens.

85

Green tree monitor (Varanus prasinus). *Photo by David Northcott, Nature's Lens.*

Black tree monitor (Varanus beccarii). *Photo by David Northcott, Nature's Lens.*

Spotted tree monitor (Varanus timorensis). *Photo by David Northcott, Nature's Lens.*

The black rough-necked monitor (Varanus rudicollis). *Photo by David Northcott, Nature's Lens.*

87

Gould's monitor (Varanus gouldii). Photo by David Northcott, Nature's Lens.

Ridge-tailed monitor (Varanus acanthurus). Photo by Sean McKeown.

Crocodile monitor (Varanus salvadorii). Photo by David Northcott, Nature's Lens.

89

Argus monitor (Varanus gouldii hornii). *Photo by Bill Love, Blue Chameleon Ventures.*

Peach throated monitor (Varanus jobiensis). *Photo by David Northcott, Nature's Lens.*

90

Disorders and Diseases

Proper husbandry, with a maintenance schedule to assure good hygienic conditions, will help ensure that your savannah monitors live long and healthy lives. In addition, it is a good practice to follow proper quarantine procedures whenever a new monitor is introduced into your collection (see: Stahl 1992; Wright 1993a). Most disease results from poor initial selection, improper or inadequate husbandry, poor diet, bad hygiene, or maladaptation. Remember, too, that if escape is even vaguely probable, it will occur, and if there is any way your lizard can injure itself, it frequently will do so after an escape. Observe your lizards, think about prevention, and be ever on the lookout for potential trouble.

Olson (1992) recommends the following items be part of a "monitor medicine cabinet" and I concur:
❒ Tweezers
❒ Betadine®
❒ Polysporin® (or "Triple Antibiotic")
❒ Styptic powder (to stop any bleeding)
❒ Nail scissors or clippers
❒ Monoject 412 or some similar item (a curved tube-syringe for mild force feeding, rehydrating, and flushing the mouth)

❏ Cotton swabs

❏ Eye droppers

❏ Plastic-tipped syringes

Olson also mentions the following as "optional" items:

❏ Nutrical® (high-calorie veterinary dietary supplement)

❏ Gerber® puréed meat-based baby food

❏ Pedialyte® for rehydration (I usually use sterile saline injectable solution for this purpose).

Finally, Olson mentions the following items but with a disclaimer about consulting with a veterinarian or professional herpetologist before use:

❏ Forte-Topical® (a prescription antibiotic supplement for use with severe mouth rot or eye infections)

❏ 0.150 pyrethrin spray (Adams® or Zodiac®, to use on ticks and mites: see below)

❏ Bovine ivermectin (an anti-helminth/anti-arthropod drug)

What to Be on the Look-out For!

Try to catch any ailment early. Often, when captive monitors are so obviously ill that immediate attention is needed, a disease will have progressed to the point where it cannot easily be successfully treated by a veterinarian. Thus, many lizards sick enough to merit a veterinarian's attention do not often survive. To discover a possibility of disease early, develop a "quick-check" method which will eventually become automatic and will allow for the recognition of any disease or other disorder as early as possible. It may even be a good idea to have "routine lab tests" run on the animals in your collection (Cauble 1992a) Check for:

a. General responsiveness/alertness. Is your monitor acting in any way abnormal? Is it unusually sluggish? Is it not feeding? Is it vomiting?

b. Breathing. Does your monitor gape much of the time? Does it occasionally forcibly expel air? Does mucus collect at the edge of its mouth or nostrils?

c. **Mouth area.** Is there any apparent swelling along the rim of your lizards mouth when closed? Has any food, debris, or other foreign material accumulated along the rim of its mouth? Are any lumps visible along the upper and/or lower jaws?

d. **Eyes.** Do the eyes appear to be alert? Are they wide open or narrowed? Do the lids show any swelling? Are they unusually wet or dry? Any crust accumulating around them? Are they swollen shut? Do the eyes appear cloudy in any way?

e. **Body.** Any cuts, scratches, or swellings? Any skin disease, lumps, brownish or blackish areas, open or running sores? Swollen limbs? Any signs of paralysis? Does your monitor walk funny? Does the head tilt or is it otherwise held in an "abnormal" position?

f. **Hands and feet.** Are any toes or fingers swollen? Is the whole foot or hand swollen? Are there remains of shed skin clinging to the toes or fingers? Has a claw suddenly disappeared?

g. **Signs of watery stools.** Check for bloody stools. Are there any stains of smeared feces around the vent? Is the vent swollen? Does the animal have frequent, unusually watery stools? Has the animal failed to defecate or otherwise excrete for an unusually long time?

If you can answer yes to any of the above questions, your savannah monitor may need veterinary attention and/or some modification and improvement in husbandry.

Veterinarians

Finding a veterinarian with experience in the treatment of reptiles and other exotic animals can be difficult. Veterinarians with no experience or knowledge about reptiles and/or herpetology can, at times, do more harm than good. Check with local herpetological societies for information about veterinarians with knowledge of treating reptiles (see also Barten 1996a). *Reptile & Amphibian Magazine* publishes a Directory (*A Guide to North American Herpetology*) where the names of many veterinarians who are interested in reptile and amphibian medicine are listed (list includes some vets in foreign countries). Barring this, or if you live in an area where there may be no experienced veterinarians, you might consider the purchase of a basic and well known reference work for herpetological medicine. One of the best known and easily obtained is Fredric L. Frye's: *Biomedical and Surgical Aspects of Captive Reptile Husbandry* (1991), which is now available in a new two- volume edition from Krieger Publishing Co. (Melbourne, FL) or from TFH under the title: *Reptile Care: An Atlas of Diseases and Treatments*. The older edition (1981, VM Publishing Co.) can occasionally be purchased, but one must remember that some of the drug dosages may no longer be valid. Be that as it may, with the help of one (or more) of these references, and the willing cooperation of a local veterinarian, it is reasonable to presume that diagnosis and appropriate treatment of many reptile diseases can be accomplished. Several other references of worth are: Anonymous (1994), Cooper and Jackson (1981), Jacobson and Kolias (1988), Klingenberg (1993), Lawton (1991), Mader (1996) (my favorite), Marcus (1981), and Ross and Marzec (1984).

Common Disorders and Diseases

a. Thermal burns. These burns usually result from improperly shielding your lizard from spotlights or other excessively warm heating devices (Barten 1996c). Superficial burns will eventually heal, but scarring may result. Serious burns will require veterinary care. Be sure to protect the animal from any direct contact with a heat lamp or spotlight (set up outside enclosures or shield them). Monitor the temperatures of all hot rocks and similar such devices, modifying or removing those that are overheated. Burns may also become infected, making a bad situation far worse, but antibiotics should not necessarily be used prophylactically (Barten 1996c).

b. Nose rub (rostral abrasion). This occurs when your monitor ceaselessly rubs its snout against screen mesh or hard (such as glass) surfaces (Frye 1991; Rossi 1996). This happens because the animal is improperly housed (as mentioned earlier, screening should be avoided for the sides of monitor cages). This behavior can also occur if the cage is too small or is poorly designed. When a monitor rubs its snout, this indicates that conditions in the cage make the animal uncomfortable for some reason or another (such as the cage is too warm or cold, too bright, etc.). Sometimes the reason is not immediately obvious; for example, the animal may be trying to reach a patch of sunlight it has spotted in some inaccessible part of the room. Try to discover the reason the animal is signaling distress and correct the problem. Place your animal in conditions where these behaviors and the resulting traumas do not persist. Remember, if the monitor does not stop rubbing its snout, the trauma will become progressively worse. Early treatment with an antibiotic salve can help the wound heal and often with little scarring. In extreme cases, your lizard can cause such damage to its snout that the entire front is destroyed, and bone and teeth may actually be exposed! Catch and treat this problem early. Reptiles have no conception of glass or other transparent barriers. They often ceaselessly try to penetrate them. Frye (1991) noted that U.S. National Zoo's reptile facility placed a visual barrier of dark paint or tape on the glass front (and where ever else the animal can see through), along the lower-most few centimeters. This will inhibit pacing and rubbing. Apparently, the animals perceive a barrier and do not attempt to cross. Somewhat similar-appearing conditions may result from bites from prey items (especially live rodents) and conspecifics as well as thermal burns (Barten 1996d; Rossi 1996), so be certain to recognize the cause.

c. **Skin and foot infections.** If your monitor is kept in conditions that are too humid or wet (especially if hygiene is not the best), it could develop skin and toe infections (Frye 1991; Rossi 1996). Extreme humid conditions are inappropriate for savannah monitors because they are native to areas with hot, dry climates. These infections appear as whitish or, more commonly, brownish to blackish raised areas. The toes will usually swell as well and be stained as above. Put the animal on a dry surface (such as clean newspaper). Keep its enclosure scrupulously clean and dry and disinfect it as well. Apply topical antibiotics to the infected surfaces. Swollen toes may require veterinary treatment due to abscesses. Another problem possibly related to humidity, especially rapid and great changes in humidity, is that many savannah monitors may develop bizarre, reoccurring foot abscesses (see Balsai and Bayless 1993). These infections are peculiar because they will normally appear at about the same time of year, seemingly, every year of the animal's life. I have been told that this problem is seen in some other lizards (such as desert iguanas, *Dipsosaurus dorsalis* [Bodri, pers. comm.]) from arid climates, that are kept in more humid areas by herpetoculturists. These abscesses are time-consuming to deal with and will require veterinary help in most cases. It helps to become experienced at treating this problem if your animal shows this syndrome. I suspect it may be a form of stress induced by unfavorable climatological conditions though not all savannah monitors will manifest this problem. Perhaps, the use of a dehumidifier (when excessively humid) may help prevent this problem.

Parasites

External Parasites

Ticks: If you obtain your animal from a good and reliable source, you will probably never observe ticks on the animal. I once obtained (rescued) a specimen from a pet store that harbored a tick. When the offending arthropod was "keyed out," it was found to be a native African tick that frequently attacks monitor lizards. The treatment for ticks is fairly easy. Apply some rubbing alcohol to the tick's surface (often several applications may be needed), and soon the irritated parasite will begin to withdraw its mouth parts from your lizard. At that time, seize the obnoxious arachnid with forceps and gently, but steadily, pull it off your lizard. Save the tick for later identification by preserving it in 70% ethyl alcohol.

Apply some topical antibiotic to the area where you extracted the tick. Do not buy a specimen that is infested with ticks, but if by some misfortune you have an infested animal, you can safely treat it with a spray or powder form of some "tickacide" containing pyrethrins or carbaryl (Sevin®). Just be sure to avoid the eyes, ears, mouth, and vent area. See Klingenberg (1993) and Mader (1993, 1996) for more information about tick treatments.

Mites: Monitors are not good candidates for harboring mites, the bane of snake keepers, but they may sometimes be seen on imported animals or they may get to your lizards if you introduce an infested reptile to your collection without implementing proper quarantine procedures. Infested animals will show signs of irritation and may be seen to be rubbing up against the sides of the enclosure or soaking themselves more often than usual. Sometimes these parasites specifically attack the eyes and, if not treated, can cause severe eye infections (from excessive rubbing against objects). While pyrethrins or Sevin® can be used to treat most infestations (except those of the eye), Vapona® No Pest Strips® (2.2 dichlorovinyl dimethyl phosphate) usually will take care of the problem very well. Use a small section of strip (about 1 or 2 in.) wrapped in a small piece of nylon screen and suspend it in the cage by attaching this to a length of thin wire (such as a "twist-tie" used for closing plastic bags). Remove all water, food, cage furniture, and substrate, and leave the strip for 2 to 4 days. It may help to place a small piece of this strip in a plastic trash bag together with any cage furniture or empty water bowls. Clean and disinfect the cage. Repeat the procedure for the same length of time about 3 weeks later. Disinfect and thoroughly wash all cage furnishings before putting them back.

There is one disadvantage to Vapona® treatment. Lizards seem to be particularly prone to idiosyncratic responses to this chemical. In other words, it could prove toxic to your pet. Symptoms of a toxic reaction will often include a chronic, progressive, total paralysis of the lizard that seems to always be fatal! Prolonged or high-dose exposure to these pest strips can also cause liver damage. I once lost a beautiful Dumeril's monitor to use of Vapona®. However, this remedy is one of the most effective at eliminating mites, and most monitors I have so treated have had no ill effects. See Klingenberg (1993) and Mader (1993, 1996) for more information about mite treatments.

Internal Parasites

The usual internal parasites found to be potential problems for monitors are tapeworms, some digestive-tract-inhabiting nematodes, and a few protozoans (e.g., *Entamoeba invadens* or some coccidia). Always quarantine all new lizards and have fecal samples checked by a qualified veterinarian to identify internal parasites and prescribe the best course of treatment (see: Cauble 1992b; Frost 1992; Klingenberg 1993, 1996b; Barnard and Upton 1994; Mader 1994; Campbell 1996; Lane and Mader 1996). I always quarantine new animals and ensure that neither they nor anything from their cages ever contacts other specimens until they have been found parasite-free (internal and external). Additionally, all new acquisitions are checked with fecal samples before any drugs are given (do not treat blindly).

Nutritional Disorders

If your monitor is getting the proper diet, these problems should not appear in your animal. However, it may be appropriate to list a few potential sources of trouble.

a.   Metabolic bone disease/calcium deficiency. This will normally not be a problem with adult monitors, but it could become one if one is not careful when feeding monitor hatchlings and juveniles. Calcium deficiency is not simply a lack of available calcium because simply adding supplemental calcium will not solve the problem. The proper absorption of calcium, via the intestinal lining, is accomplished with an adequate amount of vitamin D_3 and a proper calcium:phosphorus ratio. Lizards seem to require 1 to 2 parts calcium to 1 part phosphorus. The reason why babies can be a source of trouble is because some beginning herpetoculturists may exclusively feed them crickets and/or "pinkie" mice. These are not totally balanced diets and should be supplemented with a mineral/vitamin mix. For those who use insects to feed very young monitors, I recommend consulting de Vosjoli (1990 or 1994), both of which are books, like this one, in the Herpetocultural Library Series.® One method to properly ensure good nutrition in young monitors is to get them to occasionally (about one or two times per month) eat canned cat (I prefer this) or dog food. Use poultry flavors which are more "natural" and somewhat less fatty. One of the major brands (such as Purina® or Alpo®) will be sufficient. By doing this, I have never encountered metabolic bone disease in juvenile monitors.

The usual symptoms of calcium deficiencies in lizards are "soft" jaws which may be further complicated by back and limb deformities (in juveniles), and, in adults, swollen "smooth" hind limbs, and/or swollen deformed lower jaws. The latter symptoms are indicative of a condition whereby the animal compensates for thin and weak bones by depositing spongy tissue. In monitors, this should NEVER be allowed to become a problem! For more information about this syndrome, see Frye (1991), Boyer (1996), and Donoghue and Langenberg (1996).

b. Induced thiamin (vitamin B$_1$) deficiency. This can be a problem for some monitor lizards, particularly Nile monitors or water monitors fed almost exclusively on thawed, frozen fish. If the fish is oily, steatitis (inflammation of fat, which will require vitamin E treatment) can also be a problem. The most common symptom of B$_1$ deficiency is twitching of limbs or fine muscular tremors. Muscular atrophy can result if this condition is left untreated too long. Change the diet, and if symptoms are severe, consult a veterinarian. This should not normally be a problem with savannah monitors because fish is not recommended as a frequent dietary staple (these lizards do not normally encounter this prey item in the wild). For more on this, see Frye (1991), Barten (1996b), and Donoghue and Langenberg (1996).

c. Induced biotin deficiency. A problem seen in monitor lizards that are fed largely on raw, nonembryonated, whole eggs. This is because raw egg white contains avidin which induces this deficiency (see: Frye 1991; Barten 1996b; Done 1996; Donoghue and Langenberg 1996). Change the diet to a more varied and balanced diet and avoid raw eggs because of the additional hazard of salmonellosis.

d. Obesity. If your adult monitor is overfed and inactive, it will become very fat. If this is allowed to continue, the fat may deposit in the internal organs, especially the liver, with potentially fatal results (Frye 1991; Donoghue and Langenberg 1996). Curtail overfeeding and restrict your animal's intake if it is becoming too fat. Encourage it to exercise by providing it with adequate space to move about and explore. Monitor lizards are very active in the wild and appear to patrol fairly large territories in search of food.

Respiratory Infections

Respiratory infections usually result from keeping savannah monitors (and other species) at temperatures that are not warm enough. This results in lowering the lizards resistance to infections and creates a situation where the immune system cannot function properly. Elevated mucous content is usually noted in the mouth and nostrils, and the mucus may appear somewhat foamy. In young animals, gently pressing the thumb against the throat will cause mucus to exude from the nostrils. Other early symptoms are: sluggishness, decreased or lack of appetite, and slightly labored breathing. Slight gaping and puffing of air in and out of the throat and lungs are sure indications of pneumonia. The sick lizard will spend much of its time with its eyes closed. As the disease progresses, all these symptoms will worsen and the animal will begin to spend time with its head elevated and bubbly mucus will begin to exude from the mouth and nose. If the disease is discovered early, elevated temperatures in the upper 80s to lower 90s (°F [30 to 32°C]) will help the monitor fight off the infection. If it does not improve after a few days of elevated temperature, then treatment with injectable antibiotics will be required. A veterinarian should be consulted as early as possible to determine and administer the most effective treatments and antibiotics. Drinking water must be available at all times during the course of treatment (see: Frye 1991; Barten 1996b; Murray 1996).

Gastrointestinal Diseases

Occasionally, savannah monitors may develop diarrhea, which may be discolored, foul smelling, and/or bloody. This condition can occur in imported animals and in established animals that are fed raw chicken parts or rotten prey or kept with foul water on a regular basis. Inadequate maintenance temperatures also contribute to the susceptibility to pathogens. If the symptoms persist for more than a few days, your monitor may have a serious gastrointestinal disease. Consult a veterinarian for diagnosis and treatment. Do not allow this to go untreated for long! With early diagnosis and treatment, the prognosis for recovery is usually good (Frye 1991; Barten 1996b; Funk 1996b).

Eye Diseases

According to Frye (1991), monitor lizards may be prone to juvenile cataracts, which occur most often (obviously) in young lizards. It is not clear why this should occur. One suggestion was dietary, but Frye suspects it could possibly be genetic because this syndrome does not occur in other lizards, including helodermatids, fed the suspected diet. Whatever the cause, Frye (1991) thinks this reflects a "genetic idiosyncrasy of varanids." The cataracts can vary in their severity. Some monitors appear to suffer little from this condition whereas others show virtual blindness, especially in low light. Cataract surgery could be done, but it is prohibitively expensive (Wright, pers. comm.). Additionally, it has been reported that monitor lizards may also develop "arcus lipoides corneae." This is a condition where a white band of material may partially or totally surround the cornea near the outer edge. This is apparently associated with aging and has no treatment (Frye 1991; Barten 1996b). I have, so far, not observed this syndrome in any savannah monitor, but Bayless (pers. comm.) mentions that it occurs in the desert monitor, *V. griseus*.

Maladaptation and Stress

Stress and maladaptation are problems that will be encountered by most herpetoculturists at some point. Acclimation is when an organism becomes habituated to a different, usually abnormal, climate or environment. This term is often applied to descriptions of animals adjusting to captive conditions. Whether a captive acclimates successfully will depend on housing, maintenance, temperature, general state of health, temperament, and nutrition. Generally, new captives require some time to adjust to the new environment, and captive-bred or long-term, captive-raised animals adjust faster and better to changes in captive conditions than wild-caught lizards. My experience has shown that adult, wild-caught animals are usually highly stressed by captivity and rarely adjust well to handling, many being quite difficult and even aggressive toward the keeper, for long periods or for their entire life. Some captives become so "stressed" by captivity they can fail to thrive (see: Cowan 1980; DeNardo 1990; Patton 1991; Arena and Warwick 1995; Greenberg 1995; Guillette et al. 1995; Warwick 1995).

A condition called "General Maladaptation Syndrome" seems to be characterized by three stages: alarm, resistance, and, finally, exhaustion. The alarm stage usually ensues within hours of exposure to some stress-inducing situation (e.g., captive conditions). This can have such symptoms as ulceration of the digestive tract (which may explain why many stressed reptiles lack appetite) and stimulation of the adrenal glands. When stress has become a chronic problem, the resistance stage will eventually manifest. Symptoms at this point can be hypertrophied adrenal glands, inhibited growth, and inhibited gonadal function. Interestingly, if the stress situation remains, the animal resists, and its physiology and morphology seems to almost regain normalcy. If the chronic stress becomes severe, the animal ultimately cannot regain normal function and will enter the exhaustion stage. This is usually characterized by symptoms similar to those seen during the alarm stage, and if the source of this stress is not eliminated, the animal will eventually die (Guillette et al. 1995; see also Cowan 1980; Warwick 1995).

It is unwise to purposely purchase animals in obvious poor health with the intent of salvaging them. It is also good practice to avoid the acquisition of aggressive or otherwise ferocious individuals because, though they may be seemingly in good health at the time of purchase, these animals are to eat, and their psychological and physiological stress will eventually depress their immune systems, making them candidates for disease (Frye 1991; Guillette et al. 1995; Klingenberg 1996a). These individuals will also be difficult to care for properly, both from sanitary considerations as well as when treatment becomes required for any illness. I have observed that maladapted monitors tend to appear very restless and aggressive at first. They tend to have little appetite and will eventually starve (Funk 1996a). Most appear dehydrated within a short time because they seem not to drink very often, if at all. "Exhaustion"-stage monitors may become listless and often acquire some type of infection. These animals nearly always expire.

Quarantine for New Acquisitions

It is always a good practice to quarantine new monitors brought into your collection. Wright (1993a) advises that all transport materials should be considered potentially infested with parasites and treated accordingly. This may include freezing the materials, disinfecting them, etc. The new animal should be examined as above for any potential problems, and it is probably a good idea to see a veterinarian for tests for internal parasites and treatment for any found. Wright (and McKeown 1996) recommends a quarantine period of at least 60 days (Cooper and Williams [1995] recommend 6 months!) and that new lizards should have their quarters cleaned last, and the owner should always wash after handling the new animal so as not to contaminate others. A new animal should also have its own "set of husbandry tools" (Wright 1993a). A quarantine enclosure should be large, well ventilated, and easily disinfected. Wright recommends choosing newspaper as a substrate during quarantine.

Notes on Other
Monitor Species

The Dumeril's Monitor *(Varanus dumerilii)*

David Northcott, Nature's Lens

The Dumeril's monitor is a modest-sized Southeast Asian species which Mertens (1942) claimed included two generally similar appearing subspecies *(V. d. heteropholes and V. d. dumerilii*, albeit Sprackland [1993c] suggested they should be synonymized). This species was named for the famous nineteenth century French herpetologist and zoologist, André-Marie-Constant Duméril. This species attains average adult lengths of about 4 ft (1.2 m), with occasional 5-footers (1.5 m) or larger (Turnipseed 1995), and occurs in the Malay Peninsula and parts of Indochina as well as parts of Indonesia. In the pet trade, it is often referred to as the brown rough-necked monitor. Dumeril's monitors are now becoming difficult to obtain and are rather expensive when available (easily averages between $200 and $300).

As hatchlings, Dumeril's monitors are very strikingly colored with beautiful yellow to almost orangish heads and gorgeous, alternating, broad, yellow and black stripes. As adults, this pattern dulls considerably. The species is well known for its ability to tame easily (many become "dog tame" and rarely attempt to bite, despite the very strong jaws) and adapts very well as a captive. Dumeril's monitors are occasionally arboreal and have highly keeled tails for swimming and climbing. A rain forest species, Dumeril's monitors prefer a rather humid and warm climate, about 85 to 95°F (29 to 35°C) during the day and about 75°F (24°C) at night. To properly maintain this species, you should provide thick branches or large cork sections to climb upon (for an interesting use of cork bark sections, see Freer 1993). This species loves to soak, so provide an extra large water container (such as a large cat litter box) or some sort of self-draining pool setup. Most individuals will regularly defecate in the water, making cage cleaning relatively easy.

Free-ranging *V. dumerilii* are fond of crabs (Krebs 1979; Losos and Greene 1988) and mollusks though captives will take a variety of foods including mice, fresh fish, shellfish, and insects. This species grabs its prey and crushes it in the jaws and rarely resorts to the more typical "prey-shaking" behavior seen in other monitor species. Additionally, this species has a fondness for disemboweling its prey, particularly mice (Balsai, pers. observ.). In my opinion, *V.*

dumerilii makes one of the best captive monitors, perhaps even better than the savannah monitor, if you can provide the proper conditions. Dumeril's monitors have rarely been bred as captives. Sprackland (1992) noted that males can become restless in July and August and prowl their quarters day and night. It is, thus, conceivable that the placement of a female in the male's quarters at this time might result in mating behavior. The first reported captive breeding I could find was in 1988 by the Buffalo Zoo (Radford and Paine 1989) though it only occurred once. Mating was successfully induced for these animals by modifying the light cycle from 12 hours to 24 hours (continuous). Mating occurred over a period of 3 days, and 14 eggs were laid about 33 to 37 days postmating in damp sphagnum moss. Another Dumeril's monitor was hatched on September 4, 1994 at the Birmingham Zoo after incubating for 214 days (75 to 84°F [24 to 29°C]). It was the only one of four to hatch and was the result of a successful captive breeding that began with a copulation in early December of 1993 and oviposition in February 1994 (Conners 1994). The size for the Birmingham hatchling was not reported, but the Buffalo animals averaged about 7 in. (179 mm) in total length (TL), and their average weight was about 0.6 oz (17.3 g). The eggs averaged about 1.1 in. (27.4 mm) and 0.6 oz (17.3 g) (Radford and Paine 1989). Recently, a 10-year-old female laid 21 fertile eggs at Zoo Atlanta (Fost 1995) between October 17 and 21, 1994. Fifteen hatched between May 3rd and 4th, and some were "helped out of their eggs" (Fost 1995). The eggs were incubated between 82 and 84°F (28 and 29°C), and better success (100% hatched) was achieved using vermiculite:water (5:6 ratio by weight) than when using vermiculite:water (5:8 ratio by weight) where only about 88% hatched. The use of damp soil for an incubation substrate had a 100% failure to hatch score. This is the largest hatching of *V. dumerilii* in a North American zoo (Fost 1995).

The Mangrove Monitor *(Varanus indicus)*

Paul Freed

This is a species which, according to Mertens (1942), consists of three somewhat similar-appearing subspecies *(V. i. spinulosus, V. i. indicus,* and *V. i. kalabeck* [now apparently *V. doreanus,* a separate species (Böhme et al. 1994)]) that are distributed throughout Australasia, particularly northwestern Australia, New Guinea, the Indo-Malayan archipelago, and some of the islands in the Western Pacific, including the Solomon Islands and the Marianas (where, on Guam, it is reported as declining in population [McCoid et al. 1994]). It seems to occur wherever the Asian water monitor is not found (Balsai 1991). *Varanus indicus* is suggested to inhabit some of these Pacific Islands as a result of human introductions (Fulbeck 1947; Uchida 1966; McCoid 1993; McCoid and Hensley 1993). Presently, it also seems that *V. karlschmidti* is actually *V. i. jobiensis* (Sprackland 1993a) though Böhme (1991b) elevates this monitor to *V. jobiensis,* a separate species. Böhme (1991b) also states that the validity of *V. i. spinulosus* may be doubtful. The species name *"indicus"* means from or out of India, which Sprackland (1992, 1993b) suggests may refer to the "East Indies." It inhabits estuarine mangrove areas, monsoon vine forests,

semi-open areas, and thick forests. McCoid and
Hensley (1993) noted, however, that *V. indicus* is
found in areas with no permanent bodies of water on
the island of Guam and that most of their observations of this lizard occurred away from water.
Mangrove monitors are often reported basking on
branches overhanging water and will hide inside
hollow limbs and tree trunks. This is another moder-
ate-sized monitor, reportedly reaching a length up to
4.9 ft (1.5 m) though most imports seldom exceed 2.5
to 3.5 ft (up to 1.1 m). This animal has beautiful
colors, with the top and sides usually a dark olive to
blackish-green and speckled with small yellow to
yellow–orange spots. The belly is largely whitish or
whitish-yellow with very small blackish spots,
almost the reverse of the dorsal pattern.

Mangrove monitors are highly carnivorous and,
in the wild, feed on virtually any vertebrate prey
they can catch as well as invertebrates, including
crabs (although this may not be true for *V. i.
spinulosus*, which only readily accepts fish, according
to Sprackland [1993a]). They are also very fond of
eggs. The juveniles will devour insects, but small
individuals are noted to take relatively large prey,
and large individuals are noted to tend to take many
small items (Losos and Greene 1988; McCoid and
Witteman 1993). Mangrove monitors have voracious
appetites, and I have found they will readily accept
adult mice. In fact their appetites are among the best
I have seen in monitors, and they are one of the few
species that may attempt to eat, even when ill.
Nelling (1995) claims they can be cannibalistic
though it is not clear whether this is restricted only to
eggs and/or juveniles. Caution is nonetheless justi-
fied.

I am particularly fond of this species, despite its
somewhat "skittish" behavior as a captive, though,
perhaps, this behavior is because all the specimens
obtained are wild-caught adults. This monitor
spends a lot of time hiding in the substrate and does
not seem to move about much. It climbs well and

should be provided with branches to climb upon. This species is said to frequent water and definitely enjoys long soaks (like most monitors, this one will defecate in the water). This monitor should be maintained similarly to the Dumeril's monitor. The mangrove monitor has very powerful claws (almost like a raptor's) and rather large teeth, so special care should be taken when handling. This species is also infamous for defecating as a defense mechanism when handled (so keep that vent away from your clothing). In addition, the mangrove monitor moves remarkably fast and is a notorious escape artist! This species is considered to be among the most intelligent of monitors (Hediger 1985; Sprackland 1992) although I prefer to claim this for the Gould's monitor (see below). Most, if not all, imported specimens are apparently from the Solomon Islands (and possibly Guam).

Kukol (1993) reported a case where a captive laid five separate clutches of infertile eggs. I have also observed this phenomenon (infertile egg laying) with my animals, each time in early spring (January or February). Records exist for observations of breeding by "wild" specimens on Guam (Wikramanayake and Dryden 1988; McCoid and Hensley 1991, 1993; McCoid 1993). Their reproduction seems to be timed for the rainy season (mid-July to mid-November) and may be to ensure adequate food for the hatchlings. These lizards have a pronounced sexual dimorphism, at least on Guam (Wikramanayake and Dryden 1988; McCoid and Hensley 1991, 1993). Although no records of egg size/weight, incubation period, or hatchling size/weight are reported for free-ranging mangrove monitors, clutch size was reported to be small (one to five eggs [McCoid 1993]); however, this may not be true, at least for captives (Kukol [1993] reported that her animal laid 9 or 10 eggs).

However, a report of captive breeding for *V. indicus* was given by Chris van Kalken (1993) of the Dutch Varanid Association. He noted that copulation occurred shortly after the male and female were placed together. Six eggs were laid and removed for incubation (because the male had eaten an earlier clutch). After five months incubation (incubation temperatures not reported), four young hatched nearly simultaneously. They were about 9.8 in. (25 cm) long and were black with pale yellow dots and pinkish-red throats. Although some *V. indicus* hatchlings may have a bit of blue on the tail (and this "father" did), these juveniles did not. On one day during incubation, the incubator was noted to malfunction and the temperature rise to 104°F (40°C) for several hours; however, this did not seem to harm these eggs at all. Wesiak (1993) also submitted a captive breeding report in which one juvenile survived. The Philadelphia Zoo obtained two mangrove monitors from Guam in 1984 (one in May, the other in July). In 1988 the female (who laid a total of 20 eggs over a span of 7 years, but only 2 were viable) laid 2 eggs about 1 day apart (January 21 and 22), and these hatched in August (one on the 8th and one on the 11th). The smaller hatchling weighed about 2.2 oz (62. 5 g), but no actual lengths were given. These hatchlings were alive in 1993 when all mangrove monitors at the Philadelphia Zoo were shipped to another zoo and are probably still alive (Gannon, pers. comm.). Little other information was available at this time concerning this captive breeding, but it appears to be the earliest record for mangrove monitors available.

The Nile Monitor *(Varanus niloticus)*

Paul Freed

This is, perhaps, the largest lizard found in Africa (up to 6.5 ft [1.99 m; Haagner et al. 1993], with the largest being about 8 ft [2.4 m; Haacke 1995]). Nile monitors are found throughout sub-Saharan Africa, along the Nile River (for which it is named) into Egypt, as well as over much of the rest of Africa along rivers and other aquatic habitats, along sandy and tree-covered banks. Most specimens for the pet trade are imported from Kenya, Nigeria, and Togo (Luxmoore et al. 1988; Bayless 1991). They show striking and somewhat variable color patterns (depending on the region of origin) and were classi-fied as having two major subspecies by Mertens (1942): *V. n. niloticus* and *V. n. ornatus*. These monitors are semiaquatic (have a highly keeled tail), but spend the early part of their day sunning on rocky outcrops, tree stumps, and sandy or muddy islets. They are active, voracious predators on crabs, mollusks (especially snails), frogs, fish, reptiles, birds, and small mammals and are a major and notorious predator upon Nile crocodile eggs (as well as other reptile and bird eggs). These animals will flee when threatened (in the case of captives, this means when attempting to handle them) and will probably lash with their tails and attempt to bite when cornered (in the case of captives, this means when attempting to pick them up) (Wright 1993b).

Nile monitors can be among the most wary and aggressive monitors, and many do not tame (especially, though not exclusively, wild-caught adults). This species is not recommended unless you are willing to spend plenty of time taming it (see Naclerio [1993, 1994] for tips on how to tame Nile monitors). The initial selection of your Nile monitor will be critical (preferably hatchlings or young animals), and frequent handling of an initially tame specimen may be essential. Nile monitors are one of the most commonly available monitors, second only to the savannah monitor. They generally fare well in captivity. These lizards are **very** powerful and require great respect (see Wright [1993b] for tips for handling these lizards).

Varanus niloticus are fairly rough in texture, and the adults range from grayish-brown to dark olive brown on top of the head and back. This ground color is mottled with scattered dark blotches and pale yellow spots and/or bands on the head, back, and limbs. The belly and throat are pale with some black bars. Juveniles are beautifully colored with black and yellow. It can be common for pet stores to confuse this species with the more desirable Asian water monitor (*V. salvator*). The easiest way to distinguish the two is to note the position of the nostrils. Nile monitors have their crescent-shaped nostrils located high, but somewhat laterally on the snout whereas the water monitors have them much closer to the tip of the snout, more toward the top than the sides, and they are round. Nile monitors can be kept like the savannah monitors, except that this species will require a large water container for soaking. It is a good idea to provide hide boxes and branches for climbing (Wright 1993b). A filtered or easily drained pool is highly desirable when keeping this species (see Naclerio [1990] for a method of constructing an inexpensive "water hole").

Nile monitors have been studied from time to time in the wild. Branch (1991) reported that males are territorial, so the herpetoculturist should be aware of this should several unsexed animals be caged together (Wright 1993b; but see Naclerio 1993). Males engage in violent combat that includes clawing, lashing of tails, and biting, as each combatant circles the other (Branch 1991; Bayless 1992a). Copulation among Nile monitors is also not a very gentile affair, though this is pretty much the case among most monitor species.

The time of year for egg laying for free-ranging Nile monitors is uncertain. Cowles (1930) postulated January and February, with occasional "earlier and later lots." Branch (1988) hypothesized, however, that these lizards oviposit in August and September whereas the Minolta Aquarium and Reptile World in Ontario noted that their captive female deposited her eggs in late April. This animal piled up her bedding into a nest (Enright 1992) whereas in the wild, these lizards are known to place their eggs in termite nests (Cowles 1930). The duration of incubation is determined by temperature and humidity, and Branch (1988) claimed that in the wild, eggs may require as much as a year to hatch. However, artificially incubated eggs kept at 86°F (30°C) will hatch in 129 to 175 days. Sprackland (1989, 1992) reported that eggs can be incubated in vermiculite at 65 to 70% humidity and somewhere between 79 and 88°F (26 and 31°C). Branch (1988) noted that neonates are about 7.9 to 12.9 in. (20 to 33 cm) in length and weigh 0.81 to 1.16 oz (23 to 33 g) when emerging from termite nests, which Cowles (1930) noted occurs a few days post hatching. Cowles also noted that the eggs are elliptical in shape and average 2.4 in. (6.15 cm) in length and 1.4 in. (3.45 cm) in diameter. He also noted that fertile eggs are firm, slightly turgid, and feel "hard to the touch" (Cowles 1930). Patterson and Bannister (1987) reported that Nile monitors lay between 20 and 60 eggs.

The Tree Monitors *(Varanus prasinus and V. beccarii)*

Varanus prasinus

The green tree or emerald monitor (*V. prasinus*) consists of two color morphs (originally designated subspecies by Mertens [1942]): One is the type usually referred to as the green tree monitor and commonly shows narrow black cross banding whereas the other, called *"V. p. kordensis"* by Mertens (1942), is also green, but with a black net-like pattern which forms close-knit, indistinct concentric rosettes (Sprackland 1991c). Cogger (1992) claims that *V. prasinus* is found in Australia though Wilson and Knowles (1988) suggest that green forms of this species may be confused for *V. indicus* "in poor lighting conditions." Both Cogger as well as Wilson and Knowles note that this species can be blackish in Australia, and Wilson and Knowles state that all Australian variants of this species are black except for the area from the snout to the eyes, which is pale bluish green. Sprackland (1991c, 1992) believes this Australian variant is actually a new species, which he has named *Varanus teriae* (name adopted in Cogger 1992). The beautiful green variants are found in New Guinea and on some of its offshore islands (Sprackland 1992). The specific name *prasinus* refers to the green hue of this lizard whereas *V. beccarii* was named after an Italian explorer and naturalist in New Guinea, Odouardo Beccari (Sprackland 1992). *Varanus beccarii* is all black and is the largest of the tree monitors (Sprackland 1991b,c, 1992). Another black species was described by Mertens (1950) as *V. prasinus* bogerti and by Sprackland (1991c) as *V. bogerti*. It may be possible that *V. bogerti* is actually an allopatric racial variant of *V. beccarii*. Both of these black varieties are found in New Guinea or its associated islands.

These tree-dwelling lizards inhabit vine, monsoon, palm, rain, and mangrove forests. They are highly arboreal and dwell mostly high up in the canopy. Tree monitors all have a prehensile tail, and somewhat sticky, soft, black-colored tissue on the soles of their feet. They are believed to be related to the mangrove monitor *V. indicus* (Sprackland 1991c). These monitors are relatively small, averaging 1.5 to 3 ft (0.5 to 0.91 m) TL. Tree monitors seem to feed almost exclusively upon insects and other terrestrial arthropods. They also take small lizards (such as geckos and skinks) and small birds and their eggs, some fruits, strips of beef, and canned dog or cat food on occasion. These lizards also apparently can adjust to hand-feeding (Sprackland 1994). Tree monitors require a setup that allows them ample area to climb (at least 5 ft long by 3 ft wide by 5 ft tall [1.5 m ∞ 0.9 m ∞ 1.5 m] for a pair [Sprackland 1994]), which means providing them with branches or small trees like that for the prehensile-tailed skink (see de Vosjoli 1993; Balsai 1995). They will need temperatures and humidity (above 65%) like the Dumeril's monitor. Tree monitors are often considered difficult to keep and are very active and nervous (so be sure to provide shelters for hiding). These lizards live almost exclusively in the canopy of forests, so shade and thermal gradients for these lizards are essential (Barker 1984; Sprackland 1994). The terrarium at the Dallas Zoo is spray-misted twice per week to ensure adequate humidity (Barker 1984). Be sure to drop the temperature at night (from, say, a daytime high of 85°F [29.4°C] to as low as 65°F [18.3°C]). These monitors do not seem to enjoy soaking (Sprackland 1991b). Tree monitors are expensive (rarely below $500 per animal) and often arrive highly stressed and full of parasitic and or bacterial infestations (Sprackland 1992, 1994). A thorough veterinary exam is usually a good idea for each new tree monitor purchased.

The Dallas Zoo was the first to breed the emerald tree monitor in 1978 (Barker 1984; Card 1994c), and this success was followed in 1992 by the Fort Worth Zoo (Pfaff 1992) and also in 1991 by the Riverbanks Zoo with *V. beccarii* (Wanner 1991). Emerald tree monitors apparently have a "hemibaculum" or hemipenal skeleton, so radiography will assist in sexual determination (Card 1994c).

At Dallas, increased misting (in September 1977) may have resulted in the initiation of courting behavior by *V. prasinus* (in December 1977; Barker 1994). A nesting area was provided for the gravid female, and she eventually laid three eggs in April of 1978. At the other two zoos, breeding was stimulated by subjecting the pair to a 24-hour photoperiod: Riverbanks Zoo used a 24-hour period between March 15 and April 30, 1991, and Fort Worth used this same tactic between November 5, 1990 and January 5, 1991. Two eggs were laid by the Riverbanks female, and six eggs were deposited by the Fort Worth animal. Dallas and Riverbanks each got one surviving hatchling whereas Fort Worth got two. Interestingly, Dallas had breeding success for the two following years, but the female ate the clutches. The Dallas zoo successfully bred *V. beccarii* in 1991 and noted that the female aggressively defended her clutch from the male, so much so, that he was removed from the enclosure (Garrett and Peterson 1991). Carlzen (1982) reported a mean clutch size for the green tree monitor of about five eggs, with a range of three to seven eggs. He also reported an incubation period of 57 to 70 days at temperatures of between 80.6 and 91.4°F (27 and 33°C). Horn and Visser (1991) gave an average weight of 0.35 oz (9.9 g) for the eggs and an average size of 1.77 ∞ 0.83 in. (4.5 ∞ 2.1 cm). The Dallas Zoo eggs weighed between 0.39 and 0.41 oz (11 and 11.5 g) (Barker 1984). Incubation times reported by the zoos for *V. prasinus* were between 164.5 and 188 days (temperature given by Dallas Zoo was 86 to 91°F (30 to 32.8°C), and the incubation time for *V. beccarii* was reported to be 156 to 161 days (unfortunately, no temperature given).

Black Rough-necked Monitor
(Varanus rudicollis)

Paul Freed

This is a very interesting and rather bizarre-looking monitor from the Malay Peninsula, Borneo, and other islands in the immediate vicinity. Black rough-necked monitors, *V. rudicollis* (the specific name literally means rough neck [Sprackland 1992]), reach an average length of about 4 ft (1.2 m) and tend to be arboreal. Wild-caught adults may not thrive (though this may be due to heavy parasite loads), but very young specimens often do reasonably well. As a rule, this is not a very aggressive species (though I have had reports of a few aggressive animals [Bayless, pers. comm.]). Adults are largely black, with a few yellow crossbands, and have very narrow, long, almost bird-like heads. They have very long necks with large, narrow, sharply keeled nuchal scales. These lizards are very distinctive in appearance and, though sometimes confused with Dumeril's monitors, are nonetheless easily distinguished from the latter monitor species (by color, scale shape, and general body and head morphology). Sprackland (1992) claims this species, as well as the Dumeril's monitor, can become thanatonic (feign death) when disturbed. I have not observed this behavior in any of my captives of either species, however, and neither has Bayless (pers. comm.) observed this for his captive *V. rudicollis.*

Black rough-necked monitors feed upon terrestrial arthropods and microhylid frogs in the wild (Losos and Greene 1988) and should be fed insects, earthworms, small lizards, and frogs as captives (some may take shrimp, and Bayless [pers. comm.] claims they are very keen on cockroaches). In the wild they have been known to use their tongues in an ant-eater-like fashion to ingest small insects (Sprackland 1992). Sprackland (1992) recommends against the use of mice and baby chickens as a staple diet for this species because of their "fragile" snouts and the propensity for constipation or vomiting by these lizards kept on this type of diet (Bayless [pers. comm.] disagrees with this, however).

This species requires a setup similar to the Dumeril's monitor and needs something to climb upon (also include some type of cover or retreat). A large bowl should be included for soaking and drinking. All imported specimens should be checked and, if necessary, treated for flagellate protozoans as well as nematodes and trematodes. Sometimes the difference between establishing in captivity and death is simply a treatment with Flagyl® (metronidazole). Some herpetoculturists suspect that this species may be social (de Vosjoli [pers. comm.] and Bayless [pers. comm.] albeit Bayless notes that only solitary individuals have been observed in the wild). If this is true, then keeping two animals together may be beneficial.

Black rough-necks have bred and laid eggs in captivity (Horn and Visser 1989; Bayless 1992b; McGinnity 1993). Recently, copulations were observed at the Nashville Zoo on numerous occasions resulting in at least 30 to 40 eggs over a period of several months (McGinnity 1993). Typical individual clutch size tends to be no larger than 16 eggs, with smaller numbers, say, 1 to 6 eggs being more common (Zimmermann 1986; Horn and Visser 1991; Bayless 1993). Incubation time and temperatures ranged, on average, from 180 to 193 days at 82.4 to 86°F (28 to 30°C) Hatchlings were between 9.5 and 10.2 in (240 and 260 mm) and weighed between 0.67 and 0.78 oz (19 and 22 g) (Zimmermann 1986; Horn and Visser 1991).

The Crocodile Monitor *(Varanus salvadorii)*

David Northcott, Nature's Lens.

This monitor also goes under the name of Papuan monitor and hails from the jungles of New Guinea. The specific name *salvadorii* is derived from the name of the Italian ornithologist, naturalist, and explorer of New Guinea (during the 1880s), T. Salvadori (Sprackland 1992). Mertens (1962) believed this species to be "von monotypischen Gattunge" (in a monotypic [sub] genus), and they are rather unique in several ways. These monitors have a peculiar tail for a monitor, in that it is at first cylindrical where it attaches to the body, and, as it continues, the tail becomes somewhat triangular, with a low double keel along the upper surface. The tail is also exceptionally long, much longer than the rest of the body (about 210–240% according to Sprackland [1992]). They have distinctive heads, which end with peculiarly bulbous noses. The teeth are very long and straight and weakly curved only near the tip (Mertens 1962). This is a very large species that can reach 10 ft, 7 in. (3.23 m) to 15 ft, 7 in. (4.75 m) TL (Wood 1982), exceeding the Komodo monitor (*V. komodoensis*) for length, though the Komodo monitor is much more robust and heavier in build. The Papuan monitor is olive–brown to dark blackish-brown with yellow spots. "Crocodile" monitor seems almost a misnomer (albeit Bayless [pers. comm.] feels this may actually refer to its huge teeth), considering that this lizard is largely arboreal, spending most of its time in the upper canopies of jungles.

Papuan monitors have a peculiar bulbous nose that may be for poking around under bark sheets to seek out invertebrates and smaller lizards and snakes as prey. In fact they have been suggested to specialize in foraging for the larger insects and other arthropods, bird eggs, fledglings, and other small arboreal vertebrates (Sprackland 1992). However, this does not explain why these lizards have such long, pointed, sharp teeth. Perhaps they actually forage for larger, feathered prey, in a manner similar to the green tree pythons and boas. They may even prey on naked-tailed rats (Anonymous 1993) or bats (Bayless 1994b), and there are several reports of captive lizards "eagerly" accepting rodents as food (Bayless, pers. comm.).

Varanus salvadorii is apparently uncommon and commands very high prices (often $1000 or more) although they can occasionally be found at some herp shows for around $800. They require a room-sized enclosure that would best be designed like the setup for tree monitors (Sprackland 1992).

Sprackland also suggests that the vivarium should be drier than that for water monitors. Large branches should be provided for climbing. This species is not a good choice, unless you can provide it with the large amount of space (including vertical) it requires. They have incredibly long tails, which they may use as weapons (though they were probably designed to balance this giant climber), and can inflict deep, nasty bites that usually require stitches. The only record I have seen, at this time, for the captive breeding of this species was cited by Bayless (1994b) for the Gladys Porter Zoo in February 1992. A single hatchling resulted, and it is still alive as of this writing.

The Asian Water Monitor *(Varanus salvator)*

David Northcott, Nature's Lens

This popular species is often called the Malayan water monitor. The specific name salvator means preserver or savior, and Sprackland (1992) notes that this may have some religious significance. It is similar in appearance to the Nile monitor (see section about Nile monitor), so take care to be able to distinguish the two species. Mertens (1942) designated six subspecies (though as many as 12 have since been described [Strimple, pers. comm.]): *V. s. salvator* (the most common), *V. s. togianus* (the rarest [Bayless, pers. comm.]), *V. s. marmoratus*, *V. s. cumingi* (the one with a bright yellow or orange head and neck area), *V. s. nuchalis*, *V. s. scutigerulus* (specimen was actually a *V. rudicollis* [Mertens 1950]), and *V. s. andamanensis* (Mertens 1963). It is perhaps, the most ubiquitous monitor lizard in Asia, and ranges from Sri Lanka, India, Indochina, south China, the Malay Peninsula and the various islands of Malaysia, the Philippines, and New Guinea, to other islands in the Indian Ocean and South China Sea; essentially wherever the mangrove monitor (*V. indicus*) and Timor monitor (*V. timorensis*) are not found (Balsai 1991; Bayless, pers. comm.). As with mangrove monitors, this species can be found in and around brackish environments (Smith 1935; Erdelen 1991) as well as freshwater habitats.

As hatchlings, these lizards are black above, with large and small yellow "ocelli" arranged in a transverse series. They have yellow and black bars along the sides of the snout and lips, and a fairly wide black transverse bar runs across the eye to behind the ear. The limbs have yellow–white spots on black. The belly is yellow with narrow, often V-shaped black bands. As a rule, when these lizards mature, the markings become less distinct, with adults often appearing dark blackish-olive above with indistinct yellow or white spots.

Water monitors can grow to rather large sizes, occasionally achieving total lengths of 6 to 7 ft (about 2+ m) though Sprackland (1992) claims they can grow to 9 ft (2.7 m) and weigh 150 lb (61 kg)! Most, however, fully mature at total lengths of 3.5 to 5 ft (1.1 to 1.5 m). Their tails tend to be slightly longer than their bodies. On average, animals between 3.5 ft (1.1 m) and 5.4 ft (1.65 m) TL may be between 3 and 6 years old (data from Vogel, interpreted in: Erdelen 1991). This species is highly aquatic and will benefit from a container to soak and/or swim in. Water monitors can be kept in setups like that for Dumeril's monitors or Nile monitors, but must be provided with larger enclosures, at least 6+ ft (1.8+ m) long and 4+ ft (1.2+ m) wide (depending upon the lizard's size). This species will climb to some degree though not like crocodile monitors, tree monitors, or black rough-necked monitors. They will eat a variety of vertebrates (including fish), large insects and other terrestrial arthropods, crustaceans, and some mollusks, fruit (Bayless pers. comm.), and, in the wild, will also feast on crocodile and turtle eggs and even turtles. Gaulke (1991) reports that this species does not seem to suffer ill effects from eating the "pest" anuran *Bufo marinus*! In captivity they fare well on rodents and most other foods commonly offered as "regular" items in a monitor's diet. If acquired as small specimens, they can usually be readily tamed, and "dog-tame," adult, captive-raised water monitors are not uncommon, although freshly wild-caught, large, adult specimens generally are ferocious and formidable. These lizards are not as easy to obtain as they were 7 to 10 years ago and are significantly more expensive.

Strangely, for as wide-ranging as this species is, little work has been done on its ecology (Daltry 1991). This is unfortunate because this species may be in serious decline in at least some of its range (Whitaker and Whitaker 1980; Das 1989). In Daltry's (1991) study of the social hierarchy of water monitors, she derived some important information for captive management of this species. She noted that aggression among monitors during social status interactions results in high levels of stress, particularly for those that are the smallest and lowest ranking members of the hierarchy. Further, gender is not a factor in these interactions (similarly noted by Hairston and Burchfield [1992] for captive animals at the Gladys Porter Zoo). Moreover, some of Daltry's study animals typically had low weight increases and often had serious disruptions to their thermoregulatory behavior. In fact, one of the juveniles in her "study group" died from injuries resulting from "social status attacks" (Daltry 1991). Daltry recommends keeping densities of animals housed together on the low side and not caging animals of greatly disparate sizes together! She further noted the importance of hiding areas and large bodies of water as an escape route for lizards subjected to aggression. She also concluded that regular and frequent feedings (albeit not enough to allow obesity) should reduce the aggression threat. Hairston and Burchfield (1992) note that they keep their male and female animals separate due to their "savage feeding responses."

Records of breeding and egg laying exist for both wild (Anonymous 1978; Biswas and Kar 1981; Andrews and Gaulke 1990; Erdelen 1991) and captive (David 1970; Anonymous 1978; Acharjyo and Mobapatra 1989; Horn and Visser 1989; Sprackland 1989; Andrews 1991; Ettling 1992; Hairston and Burchfield 1992; Graham 1994) water monitors. Hairston and Burchfield (1992) mentioned the importance of ensuring that the lizards not be obese (they keep their lizards lean, "similar to those in the wild") and that the cages be well lit, warm, and humid, though soaking pools are not essential. These authors also noted that the females can show a predisposition for reproductive tract infections. They also observed that males may actually injure the females during mating, in particular by inflicting serious bite wounds. Mating has usually been observed about a month before the eggs are laid. In the wild, these lizards have been observed to lay their eggs in termite nests (Biswas and Kar 1981), burrows, and hollow tree trunks (Anonymous 1978; Erdelen 1991). Graham (1994) reported that nest guarding was observed with captive animals at the Sedgwick County Zoo (Hairston and Burchfield [1992] reported that females will often eat a few eggs). At this zoo, a 4-ft (1.2 m) SVL, 42-lb (19 kg), wild-caught male was mated to a 2.5-ft (76 cm) SVL, 15-lb (6.8 kg), wild-caught female. About a month after mating, this female deposited her eggs in a burrow she had excavated. As she excavated the nest, the female would behave defensively and rebuild it after it was disturbed. This female was successfully mated several times thereafter, and at least three clutches of 13 eggs were recovered. Sometimes, the female would attack the male after introduction, so these attempts must be monitored for aggression between the couple.

Water monitors lay between 3 and 25 eggs, with an average of 15. Egg lengths vary between 2.6 and 3.2 in. (6.7 and 8.1 cm) in length and 1.3 and 1.7 in. (3.2 and 4.3 cm) in width (Andrews and Gaulke 1990; Horn and Visser 1991; Sprackland 1992). Eggs, which appear white, somewhat "soft-shelled," and elongated with blunt ends (Acharijyo and Mobapatra 1989), may weigh between 1.2 and 2.6 oz (33 and 72.5 g). Eggs have been incubated at temperature between 77 and 91.4°F (25 and 33°C) and have hatched between 6 and 8 months later (Andrews and Gaulke 1990; Horn and Visser 1991; Hairston and Burchfield 1992; Sprackland 1992; Graham 1994). Hatchlings can be between 7.1 and 12.6 in. (18 and 32 cm) in length and weigh 0.88 to 2.08 oz (25 to 59 g; Andrews and Gaulke 1990; Sprackland 1992). Hatchlings will commence eating after 3 days and will take insects and "pinkie" mice (which should be supplemented with calcium) and fish, both live and dead (Hairston and Burchfield 1992; Sprackland 1992). Hairston and Burchfield (1992) noted that different temperatures for incubation produce enough variation between the sexes of the hatchlings to be noticeable. They also reported that they have had good results incubating eggs in a 2/3 vermiculite to 1/3 peat moss mixture moistened with tap water in a 2:5:1 ratio. They believe the maximum safe incubation temperature for these lizards is just below 90°F (32.2°C). Finally, they claim hatchlings can be sexed about 10 days post hatching by applying slight pressure to the ventral area of the tail, about 0.2 to 0.35 in. (5 to 9 mm) behind the cloaca, causing the hemipenes to evert. These authors noted that young water monitors can be housed together until they are about 1 year old.

Recently Available Australian Species

The Spiny-tailed Monitor *(Varanus acanthurus)*

Sean McKeown

Spiny-tailed monitors (sometimes called ridge-tailed monitors) are usually thought of as a "medium-sized" species ranging in size from about 2 to 2.7 ft (60 to 83 cm) TL. They are found throughout most of northern and central Australia and are occasionally available in small numbers from captive breeders. *Varanus acanthurus* resembles another Australian varanid known as Storr's monitor (*V. storri*) except that the latter is about half the size of *V. acanthurus*, is reddish, and has a somewhat spinier tail. The specific name means spiny-tailed (Sprackland 1992). Three subspecies are recognized: *V. a. acanthurus* from northwestern Australia, *V. a. brachyurus* from the rest of its mainland range, and *V. a. insulanicus* from Groote Eylandt. Their bodies usually show a rich brown (sometimes reddish-brown, especially the southern form) reticulated pattern, which encircles small, yellow spots and lines. Some spots may have several brown scales in their centers. The neck tends to have long yellow stripes instead of spots, and ventral surfaces have a pale brown or light yellow coloration. The tails are fairly round in cross section, lack a keel, and are 1.3 to 2.3 times longer than the head and body combined (Cogger 1992).

Found in arid and seasonally dry areas, spiny-tailed monitors are reported to enter termite mounds during the day (Hoser 1989). Hoser (1989) claims that the ridges and spines on the tail make this lizard difficult to dislodge from rock crevices and such, in which it hides. Losos and Greene (1988) reported that in the wild these monitors feed on insects and small lizards, and Dryden et al. (1990) noted they are "secretive sit and wait predators." As captives, these lizards accept crickets and newborn mice, seem to refuse waxworms (Murphy 1971, 1972; Thissen 1992), and should have their food dusted with powdered vitamin and mineral supplements. Thissen (1992) noted that he adds B and multicomplex vitamins to his lizards' water and feeds them insects and one mouse twice per week, 3 weeks per month. He also sprays his lizards with lukewarm water each morning. At the Dallas Zoo, these monitors are fed three times per week (Murphy 1971, 1972). Thissen keeps his lizards at 82 to 105°F (28 to 41°C) during the day and 57 to 63°F (14 to 18°C) at night. At Dallas, the ambient temperature is 81°F (27°C) and a spotlight provides an area that is 104°F (40°C). Thissen measures the humidity for his cages at 50 to 65% and provides a 12- to 14.5-hour light cycle, and Dallas Zoo reports 40% humidity with a 9-hour light cycle. Cover should be provided for these lizards as well as areas on which to climb (see Horn and Visser [1989] for other captive condi-tions). Sprackland (1992) noted that these lizards will whip their tails about when handled (which can cause skin abrasions), but they do not lash their tails in the manner that most other varanids do to dis-suade any potential seizure. Wesiak (1992) reported a bizarre incident of self-mutilation in this species.

This is the only species of monitor lizard known to have been captive bred into the third generation (Thissen 1991, 1992) and may still be the only species bred beyond the first generation (Horn and Visser 1989). Besides Thissen, these lizards have been successively bred by the Dallas Zoo (Murphy 1971) and the Frankfort Zoo (Thissen 1992). Thissen reported that males will engage in frequent "combat rituals." To promote mating, Thissen reduced the ambient temperature and the daylight period (from 14.5 to 6.5 hours per day) for about 4 months. After that, normal conditions were more or less restored, and the lizards eventually engaged in mating behavior. The female laid eggs (three to four on average) less than a month postmating. Eggs were incubated on vermiculite at 81 to 83°F (27 to 28.5°C) and 65 to 85% humidity. Average total length of the hatchlings was about 5.4 in. (13.7 cm) and average weight about 0.13 oz (3.6 g). Murphy (1971) noted that the female will excavate a burrow in damp sand to lay the eggs, and these hatch in about 4 months. King and Rhodes (1982) noted that females may begin to reproduce within the first or, more usually, the second year. They also noted that this varanid species does not show a male-biased capture ratio like most other monitor species. Thissen (1991, 1992) reported that his animals double clutched.

The Timor Monitor *(Varanus timorensis)*

The Timor monitor, often commonly called the
spotted tree monitor, is a rather small species found
in parts of northern Australia, southern New Guinea,
and, of course, the island of Timor, from which it gets
its generic name *(timorensis)*. There may be three
subspecies (Funk and Vilaro 1980): *V. t. timorensis*
(found on Timor); *V. t. scalaris* (found in northwestern
Australia, and considered by some authorities as a
full species (Storr et al. 1983, Strimple pers. comm.);
and *V. t. similis* (found in the Northern Territory and
Queensland, and in southern New Guinea). It
averages about 2 ft (60 cm) TL, and its tail length is
about 1.5 times the SVL. This lizard has a variable
pattern, but most Timor monitors appear from gray
to black on the dorsum with many white or yellow
flecks and spots. Some spots, especially the larger
ones, have black centers. These spots can either
appear somewhat leopard-like or form transverse
rows. Occasionally, the pattern may be indistinct. A
black stripe is often located along the temporal
region and may be edged, ventrally, with white.
Limbs may be spotted, and the tail is usually black or
gray with light (usually white) stripes. The tail is
round in cross section and for the most part lacks any

keel (description based on living specimens and Cogger [1992]). An arboreal monitor that ventures to the ground to feed, it can be observed in the wild basking or foraging on trunks and branches, and it will shelter in hollow limbs, holes and even under loose bark (Cogger 1992). In nature, it feeds upon insects and other terrestrial arthropods, lizards, small snakes, frogs, and small mammals (Swanson 1987; Losos and Greene 1988; Cogger 1992). The terrarium for this species, as with *V. acanthurus*, should be of "reasonable" size. Chippindale (1991) recommended one about 6.4 x 1.2 x 2 ft high (195 x 36 x 60 cm high) whereas Behrmann (1981 [1992]) used one 6.6 x 2 x 1.6 ft (200 x 60 x 50 cm). Chippindale (1991) used newspaper for a substrate (as do I) and provided branches and rocks as well as a box of dry soil for burrowing. Behrmann (1981 [1992]) used fine sand as substrate, and Zimmermann (1986) suggested "forest soil" or peat moss (half moist, half dry) as other substrate alternatives. I provide a hide box, inside which this animal hides for most of the day. Day temperatures ranging between 77 and 86°F (25 and 30°C) were used by virtually all authors consulted, and night temperatures ranged between 68 and 73.4°F (20 and 23°C). Chippindale noted his light cycle was 12 hours of light though he pointed out this was not rigorously maintained. Behrmann observed that his animals enjoyed basking under a spotlight and that they seemed to have no established hierarchy (which is contrary to the opinion of Zimmermann [1986] and, to some degree, Chippindale [1991]). All provided a "large" water bowl. Foods offered include pink and "fuzzy" mice, insects of varying kinds, earthworms, fish, canned catfood, and eggs. Most used a three-times-per-week schedule and offered vitamin and mineral supplements (once per week).

This species has been bred in captivity. Chippindale (1992) noted that the mating period is short (usually about a month) and occurred for his animals usually between the first week of January and the first week of February. He suggested that they may be regulated by an internal clock. He noted that his female laid its eggs about a month after mating (Zimmermann [1986] mentioned that about 40 days may pass until the eggs are deposited). Behrmann's female laid her eggs in August, which weakens Chippindale's suggestion of a biological clock. In all the above cases, the eggs, which appear snow-white and well formed (Behrmann 1981 [1992]), were removed and incubated at about 90%+ humidity and temperatures between 82.4 and 86°F (28 and 30°C). Emergence times varied from a low of 93 days to a high of 140 days (Behrmann 1981 [1992]; Zimmermann 1986; Chippindale 1991)., and the female will look swollen (very much like *V. acanthurus*) and seek a sandy or soil area to lay the eggs (Chippindale 1991). Hatchling sizes ranged from 3.4 to 6.0 in. (8.7 to 15.3 cm). Chippindale (1991) gave hatchling weight ranges of between 0.15 and 0.19 oz (4.1 and 5.3 g) and identified his animals as *V. t. similis*. This would support Miller's (1993) hunch that these animals are being imported from New Guinea. Behrmann (1981 [1992]) and Zimmermann (1986) mentioned that the hatchlings begin feeding after about 3 days.

The Argus and Gould's Monitors *(Varanus gouldii)*

Sean McKeown

The argus and Gould's monitors are moderately large monitors 3.9 to 5.2 ft (1.2 to 1.6 m) that look similar and, until recently, were classified as two species: *V. panoptes* (argus) and *V. gouldii* (Gould's) by Storr (1980). However, the story gets complicated, and the species that was once *V. panoptes* has now become *V. gouldii*. This reclassification now includes, in addition to all of the former *V. panoptes* subspecies, one of the former *V. gouldii* subspecies, *V. g. gouldii* (Böhme 1991a). What was once *V. g. flavirufus*, an exclusively desert-dwelling form of Gould's monitor from Australia's interior, however, has now become a new species: *V. flavirufus* (Böhme 1991a). Because *V. flavirufus* is an arid-loving form and can be distinguished from the other varieties of "Gould's" monitors by color pattern, scale patterns (presumably), habitat, and general unavailability for the pet trade (this animal is commonly called "sand monitor" although this name is sometimes appended to *V. gouldii*), it will not be discussed here. The specific name *gouldii* indicates that these lizards were named after the famous nineteenth century British naturalist and ornithologist, John Gould (Storr et al. 1983). The now-extinct specific name *"panoptes"* alludes to the color pattern, particularly the rows of spots on this lizard's dorsum (they resemble many eyes, thus, "all eyes") and refers to a giant, named Argus, with 100 eyes from Greek mythology who was made guardian of Io and was later slain by Hermes (Storr et al. 1983).

Color patterns for *V. gouldii* are somewhat variable, but the vast majority, if not all, of the argus monitors imported into the United States are from southern New Guinea, which would make them the subspecies Böhme refers to as *V. gouldii horni*. The other two subspecies, *V. g. gouldii* and *V. g. rubidus*, are Australian. The imported species is rather dark on the dorsal side, with many spots that continue as rings of spots across the belly. The far end of the tail is light in color and shows a distinctive banding (*V. g. rubidus* has a somewhat reddish color, no banding on the tail, and the tail is yellow [Storr et al. 1983]). The tail is strongly keeled except near the base, and the tail can be about 1.5 times the SVL. Nostrils are round and located near the tip of the snout.

In the wild, these lizards are said to forage over a wide area, as much as 1.2 miles (2 km), and they can commonly be seen digging up small animal burrows to extract the inhabitants (Wilson and Knowles 1988). They are known to rest in burrows (as well as tree hollows and dense litter) of their own manufacture, and they may have several burrows excavated throughout their territories (Wilson and Knowles 1988; Hoser 1989; Cogger 1992). Their burrows tend to slope and have an expanded terminal area at the base of low vegetation (Wilson and Knowles 1988). Gould's monitors are also known to be quite fast and can be seen dashing to their nearest burrow or, more rarely, up a tree, when disturbed. These lizards (as well as the other desert-dwelling species) are probably the monitor species most likely to rear up on their hind legs to get a better view of the surroundings or for defense. In fact, when threatened, they will readily rear up on their hind legs (almost kangaroo-like), arch their backs, puff out their throats, hiss loudly, and may even lunge at an aggressor if too close (Wilson and Knowles 1988; Hoser 1989; Cogger 1992). They may also rock from side to side (Swanson 1987). I have observed this "defensive" behavior often displayed by my juvenile specimen, which can also actually walk a short distance while bipedal. This particular individual is virtually fearless!

In the wild, *V. gouldii* will feed upon almost any prey they can catch, including insects and other terrestrial arthropods, small mammals, lizards and other reptiles, frogs, fish, birds, and carrion (Shine 1986; Losos and Greene 1988; Valentic 1994; Card 1995). They seem particularly adept at finding prey, even when no discernible evidence of any prey item is visible to human observers (Valentic 1994). Gould's monitors are known to be voracious feeders (Swanson 1987), and I can attest to this. These lizards will also attempt to consume incredibly large items, shaking them about until their very sharp shearing teeth slice through the food. Their jaws are quite strong, and bites from adult animals will almost certainly require medical attention. As captives, they eat nearly any sort of animal they can swallow. Mice are appropriate, and they will also take baby chickens, fish, and insects. Sprackland (1992) notes that reluctance to feed by this species is a sure sign of illness, and a visit to the veterinarian is well advised. Sprackland also notes that because this lizard is an opportunistic feeder in the wild, eating whatever and whenever it can, this habit can make it prone to over-feeding and obesity as captives.

Sprackland (1992) observed that cages must be free of any sharp edges because these monitors are especially prone to rubbing their snouts raw (be especially careful with screens with this species) and can tear the junction of the claw and toe on sharp edges. They are incredibly active, so a very large cage is appropriate and probably even necessary. In the wild they appear to forage over very large areas, with an average distance traveled of ca. 367 ft (111.6 m; Thompson 1992)! Except when sleeping, they will usually be exploring for ways to escape, so cages must be very strong and secure. They do not enjoy handling and usually thrash, claw the air, and whip their tails until placed down again. These lizards do not do anything slowly, and their frequent and sudden bursts of activity are almost bird-like and potentially "unnerving" to keepers unfamiliar with them. I strongly recommend against caging this species with any other monitor species and suggest that each individual should almost certainly be housed separately. This species will benefit from a basking area kept warmer than the rest of the enclosure. Daytime temperatures should be between 82 and 92°F (29 and 33°C), and nighttime temperatures can drop to about 70°F (21°C). These animals require a water bowl but seem never to defecate in it. These lizards display a particularly high gait when walking, with the body held very well up above the substrate. They can also leap rather suddenly, far and high. Card (1995) noted that maintaining these monitors on smooth substrates, such as newspaper, may result in overgrown and fragile claws that may break and bleed easily. So far, I have not observed this with my specimen.

Sprackland (1992) noted that this species is believed to be "quite intelligent" by many herpetologists (see also Valentic [1994] for an interesting observation). He reported that some claim Gould's monitors become accustomed to a particular feeding time, respond to the sight of a feeding dish, distinguish between people, and may even respond to their names! Although I have observed some of the above peculiarities with my specimen, response to its name, so far at least, has not been one of them.

However, the following anecdote (Balsai, pers. observ.) should suffice to convince just about anyone that this species may, indeed, be more intelligent than most or all of the others. I purchased a very young argus monitor (*V. g. horni*) from an animal dealer. The lizard was about 7 in. (17.8 cm) TL at the time. It was housed in a cage adjacent to that of a 4.5-

ft (1.4 m) boa constrictor. As described, argus monitors are almost hyperactive, and this one was no exception. It would scamper and cavort about its cage almost ceaselessly. This activity would attract the attention of the neighboring boa, which would attempt to capture the monitor by striking out at it. Of course, the boa could not get the lizard because two layers of glass separated them (they both inhabited aquaria at the time). At first, the boa's strikes would send the lizard scurrying into or behind its hide box, from which it would quickly peer out at the snake. In a very short time, this argus monitor appeared to realize that the boa could not possibly get it, and an amazing "change" in behavior occurred. From that point on (a mere couple of days after the boa first began striking), this lizard did everything in its power to encourage the boa to strike. Eventually, it would rear up on its hind legs and stare at the boa in easy view of the snake. The snake would strike, but the monitor would not even flinch! Rather, it would merely stand there and occasionally flick its tongue out at the snake. Sometimes the lizard would even fall asleep in this position! Eventually, both tired of the "game" and ignored each other, and have done so ever since.

Captive-breeding of this species was reported on a few occasions. However, because of taxonomic changes, it can be somewhat confusing as to which species is actually being described in the account. Hoser (1989) claims that Gould's monitors will extrude the hemipenes when caught, though he does not mention whether they must be adult to do this. Card (1995) observed that sexing juveniles is difficult because the hemipenes are not yet ossified (occurs by the second year of age). The reproductive season reported for *V. g. gouldii* is December to February whereas that reported for *V. "panoptes"* is February to March (Shine 1986; James et al. 1992). In the wild, the mean clutch size is reported to be between 9 and 11 eggs for *V. "panoptes"* and between 3 and 11 for *V. gouldii* (Shine 1986). The Dallas Zoo reported double clutching in *V. gouldii*, and their lizards mated in December–January and again in May (Card 1994b). In the earlier case, this coincided with the lengthening of photoperiods and "artificial rains" at this zoo. Their *V. gouldii* pairs have produced two clutches per year for two consecutive years. Eggs were laid in late March–early April for the first of the two matings whereas the May mating resulted in egg deposition in late May to mid-July. The egg sizes varied, but most were between 2.2 and 2.4 in. (5.5 and 6.0 cm) long and had a mean weight between 1.36 and 1.39 oz (38.6 and 39.4 g). The number of eggs varied between 5 and 10, and neonate total lengths varied, on average, between about 12.2 and 12.5 in. (31.0 and 31.7 cm). The neonate weights varied, on average, between 36 and 37.8 g (1.27 and 1.33 oz). An incubation time of 220 days was reported by the Dallas Zoo (Card 1993). Irwin (1986 [1991]) reported that he incubated his *V. gouldii* eggs in 1:1 vermiculite:water in a "hospital-type" incubator at 100% humidity and 86 to 89.6°F (30 to 32°C). Irwin's incubation time was 265 days, and the hatchling average total length was 10. 6 in. (27.0 cm). He also noted that his hatchlings commenced feeding after 8 days and were subject to "intragroup aggression." He fed them strips of chicken, baby mice, and dog food. His captive female dug a burrow almost 39.37 in. (100 cm) long and 8.27 in. (21 cm) deep. Bayless et al. (1994) reported another successful captive breeding. Card (1995) suggested that allowing males to "combat" will sometimes encourage otherwise "stagnant" individuals to breed. In addition, he encouraged the separation of gravid females from any cagemates (gravid females are aggressive, and conspecifics may consume the eggs) and he recommended females should be given a "nest chamber" (a 25-gallon [94.6 liter] plastic trash can filled with soil is "ideal" according to Card [1995]).

Tegus

Tegus are large teiid lizards from South America, and, despite a striking superficial resemblance (though tegu necks are much shorter), are not close relatives of monitor lizards. The name "tegu" means lizard in an Amazonian dialect (Gotch 1986; Sprackland 1992), and the specific name for one of the species, *teguixin*, is derived from tegu. *Tupinambis* (actually Tupinambas) is the name of an extinct Amazonian Indian tribe (Gotch 1986; Sprackland 1992). These lizards resemble monitors in size and general appearance, and some people may confuse them. In particular, they have tapering snouts, forked tongues, and long puissant tails (though the tails are not keeled). Mature male tegus tend to be larger and more robust than females, and old males may have jowls. Unlike monitors, these lizards can loose the tail and regrow it, and evidence of such autotomy may be common, particularly among wild-caught "golden" tegus (Balsai, pers. observ.). The tails are normally about the same length as the snout–vent length (SVL). The scales along the dorsal side of the head and along the lateral aspects of the muzzle in front of the eyes are quite large, much more so than on monitors. In addition, the rest of the body is entirely covered with somewhat small, lustrous, shiny, almost glassy bead-like scales. Tegus are heavy-bodied, strong-framed, ground-loving lizards. Their limbs are strong with sharp claws (though not nearly as talon-like as most monitors), but appear somewhat shorter when compared to their bodies than the legs of monitors are. Tegus readily dig, and captives will nearly always tunnel below the substrate. My red tegu is rarely seen above the substrate. It might be reasonably argued that tegus may fill an ecological niche in South America, similar to the one monitors fill in the areas where they are found (Laurent 1979; Tyler 1979).

The taxonomy of these lizards is a bit "confused" (Luxmoore et al. 1988). Peters and Donoso-Barros (1970 [1986]) argued for four species: *Tupinambis duseni*, *T. nigropunctatus*, *T. rufescens*, and *T. teguixin*. However, Presch (1973) argued for only two species, considering *T. duseni* to be synonymous with *T. rufescens*, and *T. nigropunctatus* a synonym of *T. teguixin*. Hoogmoed and Lescure (1975), however, disagree on *T. nigropunctatus* and propose that it is either a distinct species or at the very least, a definite subspecies of *T. teguixin*, an opinion I share. Interestingly, Langerwerf (1995) notes that juvenile black and white tegus from Argentina look more like the young of red tegus than those of black and white tegus from Columbia.. For the purposes of this book, *T. teguixin* will be subdivided into *T. t. teguixin* (commonly called "black," "white," or "black and white" tegu) and *T. t. nigropunctatus* (commonly called "golden" tegu, and which may also include the Colombian black and white tegu). *Tupinambis rufescens* is usually called the "red" tegu by the pet trade and this is what *"rufescens"* means (Gotch 1986; Sprackland 1992). Red tegus and golden tegus average about 3.9 ft (1.2 m) total length whereas black and white tegus can get even larger, on average 4.6 ft (1.4 m), and as much as 10.5 lb. (4.75 kg) (Sprackland 1992; but Luxmoore et al. [1988] note that red tegus are slightly larger than *T. teguixin*).

▲ Colombian black and white tegus are an easily maintained species and a good choice for those wanting a large lizard as a pet. Because of the potential for injury from bites and because they are powerful animals, they are generally not recommended for young children. Photo by David Northcott, Nature's Lens.

According to Luxmoore et al. (1988), the ranges of the "white" and "golden" tegu do not overlap (suggesting an argument for full species designations for these two forms) but the "red" and "white" do seem to overlap in their ranges. It has been suggested by those authors that the "red" species prefers drier habitats than the "white," and I have observed that the "red" species does seem to require somewhat hotter temperatures than the "white" and does not tolerate cooler temperatures as easily (observed for captives, Balsai, [pers. observ.]).

Luxmoore et al. (1988) gives the ranges of these lizards as follows: *Tupinambis teguixin* is widespread from eastern Argentina through Uruguay, Paraguay, Bolivia, and southern Brazil; *T. t. nigropunctatus* (which may include the Colombian black and white tegu) is widespread in northern South America and mainly to the east of the Andes, but reaches the "Isthmus of Darien" in Colombia; *T. rufescens* is found mainly in the drier areas of western Argentina, but may possibly extend through Paraguay into

▲ *The Argentine black and white tegu* (Tupinambis t. teguixin) *is considered by many to be the most desirable of the tegus. It is the opinion of a number of herpetoculturists that this species should be considered distinct from the Colombian black and white tegu and from the golden tegu, based on differences in size, skin texture and scalation, egg clutch size, and incubation time.*
Photo by Philippe de Vosjoli.

Brazil and possibly Bolivia. It can be said, then, that these lizards are found in a variety of habitats, including tropical rain forests, marshes, and arid scrubland (especially *T. rufescens*, albeit preferring the margins of ponds and rivers in these areas [Luxmoore et al. 1988]). These lizards are known to be opportunistic and hardy and may thrive in cattle-farming areas. In the more southern parts of the range, tegus may hibernate in burrows over the winter though the time spent hibernating may vary depending on location. These burrows can be as much as 1.6 to 4.9 ft (0.5 to 1.5 m) deep (Luxmoore et al. 1988). They may also select abandoned animal burrows, crevices, hollow tree trunks, and even the gaps under roots. These lizards are diurnal in habit.

Free-ranging tegus are reported to be omnivorous in the wild, eating such items as snails and other terrestrial gastropods, insects and other terrestrial arthropods, small mammals, birds (Martuscelli and Olmos [1996] report observations of a tegu raiding a nest and preying upon immature birds), and reptiles, fruits, honey, eggs (bird, caiman, and turtle), and carrion. Juveniles seem to prefer a mostly insectivorous diet. Tegus show a shift in their diets as they mature, and this is reflected in their dentition (Presch 1973), as is true of some monitors (such as Nile monitors and savannah monitors). In turn, while immature tegus may be eaten by snakes and predatory birds, the adults have virtually no natural predators except some of the predatory cats and possibly humans (Luxmoore et al. 1988). It is certainly no exaggeration to claim that these lizards are easily as important to the reptile leather industry as monitor lizards (Norman 1987; Luxmoore et al. 1988; Fitzgerald 1994). In fact, it is reported that the tegu skin trade is important to every level of the economy in Argentina and Paraguay, and the export value of this resource is at least $20,000,000, with the major importers being the USA, Canada, Mexico, Hong Kong, and several European countries (Luxmoore et al. 1988; Fitzgerald 1994)! These lizards are reported to be the most extensively hunted reptiles in South America, albeit the pet trade is a very minor contributor to this potential threat (Luxmoore et al. 1988). Cornered tegus can become quite defensively aggressive. They will display an open mouth while hissing (tegu hissing is peculiar because it consists of a series of short bursts or puffs; not at all like that of a monitor) and lashing their tails, but will take off to a protective burrow at the first opportunity.

For the most part, tegus can be kept very similarly to monitor lizards. They have many of the same requirements as captive savannah monitor lizards, except they seem to tolerate humidity better. *Tupinambis t. teguixin* and *T. t. nigropunctatus* seem to tolerate cooler temperatures a bit better than *T. rufescens*. Basking lights should be provided at all times because these lizards are known to spend time basking near their burrows. It has been my observation that if a *T. rufescens* is kept at ambient temperatures below about 75 to 80°F (24 to 27°C), it becomes very lethargic and withdrawn. It may even simulate hibernation behavior. Whether this is good or bad is, at present, undetermined. Langerwerf (1992/93, 1995) mentioned that his tegus (*T. teguixin*, which originated from Argentina) hibernated longer than any other lizard he keeps and his animals hibernate up to 7 months. Langerwerf lives in Alabama and he houses his animals outside all year long. There is an impressive photo taken by Langerwerf (1995) to show how cold it can get in winter in Alabama and that an impressive amount of snow can accumulate there.

Tegus, like monitors, are large lizards and require large spaces. These lizards can spend a large amount of time buried under the substrate or in a burrow, suggesting that they may not require quite as much space as a monitor lizard (Balsai, pers. observ.); however it is always a good idea to err on the high side. Beltz (1989) recommends not using wood chips, gravel, dirt, corn cob bedding, or the like because it may abrade the lizard's feet (though Langerwerf [1995] uses 1.5 to 2 ft of topsoil in his outdoor enclosure). She believes that these materials can lead to foot infections and the like. Beltz recommends newspaper, which is what I use. She notes that tegus enjoy hiding in the newspaper layers (Balsai, pers. observ.). Beltz observed that if males are housed together, they should be observed for potential compatibility problems though females can seemingly get along housed together with no problem. If communal housing is used (see, for example, Langerwerf's impressive outdoor enclosures [1995]), separate sleeping and feeding quarters may still be recommended. I recommend against permanently housing more than one animal together unless trying to breed them or unless an extremely large enclosure, such as Langerwerf's (1995), is used. Then, no disease or incompatibility can be a likely problem. Hall (1978) observes that tegus are not very adept as climbers (also Balsai, pers. observ.).

Many herpetoculturists, as well as I, have noted a high tendency for aggression among adult and baby wild-caught tegus. Beltz (1989) and Sprackland (1992) note that frequent handling will tame them and keep them tame. I, however, believe this may work for red tegus and black and white tegus, but have found this to be much less effective with golden tegus. I have hand-raised golden tegus and still found many to be somewhat more aggressive than the other species, despite taming efforts. They almost seem to be the "Nile monitors" among tegus. Biting tegus can be handled as per the method of Attum (1994). Always remember that tegus have very powerful bites and very strong jaws.

Tegus are usually aggressive feeders and can be fed much of the same fare as monitors. They are also known to eat fruit, and Beltz (1989) mentions a diet using mice and Purina Trout Chow® that has been soaked in water and mixed with egg yolk. Canned fruits can be added to this Trout Chow® gruel. Beltz prefers an all-mouse diet, however. Hall (1978) observed that her tegus would regurgitate vegetable food, and after several trials she discontinued the practice A captive red tegu was observed to consistently refuse various fruits offered (Balsai, pers. observ.). Fagan (1994) reported that his tegu will only eat live food, but others (e.g., Beltz 1989; Balsai, pers. observ.) regularly feed dead rodents to the adults with no trouble whatsoever. I have found that juveniles tend to prefer insects, and they can be trained to devour canned cat food (as can the adults; in fact, golden tegus seem to show a marked liking for canned poultry cat food flavors). Insect diets should be handled as per de Vosjoli (1990, 1994). As with monitors, tegu keepers must avoid overfeeding their charges and encouraging obesity. Tegus, of course, must be offered water, and a good heavy bowl should be used. Tegus will also soak in water and even sleep submerged (Olmos 1995). They are said to be good swimmers (Sprackland 1992; Olmos 1995). Sprackland observed that these lizards can be conditioned to a feeding time and schedule. He also noted that with good care, these lizards can live at least 10 to 12 years. Beltz (1989) recommends taking newly acquired tegus (presumably wild-caught) to a veterinarian for an examination for parasites. Wild-caught golden tegus seem prone to high nematode infestations (Balsai, pers. observ.).

Mercolli and Yanosky (1994) reported that the stomachs of about 70 Argentine white tegus purchased from hide hunters contained almost 70% vegetable material (fruits and seeds, mostly), about 13% invertebrates, and around 20% vertebrates. Some herpetoculturists might wonder if tegus should be given a higher vegetarian diet. However, note that Mercolli and Yanosky only received animals from one Argentine province, and they did not mention whether these lizards were captives prior to being slaughtered for their hides. They also noted that these lizards were collected between November 1990 and March 1992, but did not specify if any particular season was favored by hunters when they gathered these animals (for example, tegus may take fruit during certain times, perhaps because this is an easy food source or because other prey is less plentiful at certain times). It is my opinion that this single report, given for 70 specimens obtained from a single Argentine province, should not necessarily affect captive diets of tegus, particularly other species. Additionally, comments offered above by other experienced herpetoculturists working with tegus should be kept in mind. Langerwerf (1992/3, 1995) has had much experience with the Argentine black and white tegu and has successfully bred them multiple times, yet he did not state that he has adopted this dietary regimen despite mentioning these data collected by Mercolli and Yanosky.

Breeding tegus has, apparently, occurred on many occasions, if one believes all the "hearsay." However, actual reported instances are rather slim (breeding red tegus has apparently gone undocumented until Hurt [1995]). Certainly, the first prob-

lem confronting anyone wishing to breed captive tegus is to distinguish the sexes. Hall (1978) mentioned several attributes utilized to distinguish male and female tegus (*T. teguixin*), and, presumably, due to close relatedness, these characteristics can be applied interspecifically. Males have an "obvious hypertrophy of the jaw muscles, and the neck appears as wide as the body" (Hall 1978; Fitzgerald et al. 1991). They also tend to be somewhat larger in size, and a circumferential measurement of the tail, just posterior to the cloaca, tends to be greater. Males may also tend to show a larger number of femoral and pre-anal pores, and males usually weigh more than females. Fitzgerald et al. (1991) reported that male tegus have two "buttons" of enlarged scales in the postanal region (observed by Hurt [1995] even on immature red tegus). However, Hall (1978) notes that all the above criteria vary widely by age and condition of the individual animals and that only manual probing has proven totally reliable. In her paper, she notes that a 0.08-in. (2 mm), ball-ended,

▲ *Young Argentine black and white tegus can be raised on crickets, king mealworms, and small mice. Photo by Philippe de Vosjoli.*

147

lubricated (sterile) probe will penetrate 1.2 in. (30 mm) or more into the base of the tail of a male whereas in females it will barely reach past the margin of the cloacal flap. She also noted (1978) that similar results can be seen for probing juveniles, albeit scaled down for size.

Luxmoore et al. (1988) noted that courtship in Argentine tegus occurs in October and November (Fitzgerald et al. [1991] claim September to October for emergence of *T. teguixin*) when males emerge from their burrows first and pursue the females as they emerge. Mating usually takes place in mid-November after which the female retires to a "breeding burrow" (Luxmoore et al. 1988; Fitzgerald et al. 1991 [who claim mating occurs from September through early January for *T. teguixin* and that it begins "a few weeks later . . . depending on the start of the rainy season" for *T. rufescens*]). These burrows are usually about 1.6 ft (0.5 m) deep and 4.9 ft (1.5 m) long, and the egg chamber is furnished with a layer of dry vegetation into which the eggs are laid. Luxmoore et al. (1988) also state that some reports (see Fitzgerald et al. 1991) have claimed that the females guard the eggs until they hatch (which usually occurs in late December to early January). Hurt (1995) noted that his ordinarily very tame female *T. rufescens* showed great ferocity when guarding her eggs. Luxmoore et al. (1988) noted that *T. t. nigropunctatus* is claimed to lay their eggs in "arboreal termite nests." There is also some possibility that a second brood may be laid toward the end of the summer. This may not be unreasonable because Andre Ngo (pers. comm.) reported that he could get between one and two clutches per year from his captive golden tegus.

Hall (1978) described the mating behavior of tegus in significant detail. She noted that this behavior includes tongue flicking and "clawing" of the back and side of the female by the male. The male may also stroke the posterior of the female's head and/or the side with his snout and chin. Hall observed that when the tegu male "claws" the female, he makes jerky, almost spasmodic, head movements and flicks his tongue. He also lifts alternate hind limbs from the substratum and then replaces them, a behavior Hall terms "marching in place." This can occur when the male lies alongside the female or when he is positioned "over her dorsum" (Hall 1978). During this behavior, the male's body and tail laterally undulate in synchrony, and the female is grasped at midbody. Sometimes, the hind legs are alternately fully stretched out in the direction of the tail, instead of being raised. Hall also reported that intense feeding activity is often observed during courtship. During copulation, the male will thrust his tail rapidly under the female's tail. During this time, the male may bite the female on the neck or thoracic region, and she will respond by exhibiting vigorous side-to-side head shaking. Hall reported that mating among the tegus at the National Zoo in Washington D.C. has been seen in September through November and in February.

Langerwerf (1992/93) reported that his tegus (*T. teguixin*) reach sexual maturity at about 3 years old. He (1995) also reported that mating by his captives occurs in May and that hibernation is necessary for breeding. Langerwerf (1995) also reported that his gravid females will, given the opportunity, select nesting materials other than those already in the hole to make their nests. Fitzgerald et al. (1991) noted that among one captive population they observed, female *T. teguixin* would only mate with "large" males and that small males were rejected. In addition, the average SVL for successfully breeding males from this population was about 17.2 in. (43.8 cm), and the average weight was 8.3 lb (about 3.8 kg) whereas for females the average SVL was 15 in. (38.1 cm), and the average weight was 5 lb (2.3 kg). Fitzgerald et al. (1993) noted that male red tegus seem more vulnerable to capture in November in Argentina than in other months, and this corresponds to their mating season. In addition, they reported that female red tegus with eggs average 1.2 ft (35.8 cm) SVL, with the smallest 1.1 ft (33.0 cm). They recorded that red tegus also show a sexual dimorphism in size, and again the males are larger. Fitzgerald et al. (1993) also believe that tegus are probably about 3 years old when they reach maturity and that males seem to compete for mates and are generally more active during breeding season. Hurt (1995) observed his captive red tegus to show breeding behavior in the spring (late April and early to mid May).

Tegu eggs, which Hall (1978) described as "creamy white and ellipsoid in shape," have shells that are partly calcareous though leathery in texture. Clutch sizes vary from 2 to 54 eggs (Hall 1978; Luxmoore et al. 1988; Fitzgerald et al. 1991 [who also reported that *T. rufescens* clutch sizes are somewhat smaller than *T. teguixin.*]). Egg dimensions reported by Hall (1978, for *T. teguixin*) averaged about 1.67 in. (42.4 mm) long by 1.04 in. (26.3 mm) wide, with an average weight of 0.62 oz (17. 6 g). Hurt (1995) reported a mean egg length of 2 in. (5 cm; similar to sizes reported by Langerwerf [1995] for his black and white tegus) and a mean egg diameter of 1.25 in. (3 cm) for *T. rufescens*. Langerwerf (1995) reported a weight of about 0.7 oz (20 g) for *T. teguixin*. The mean incubation time was about 154 days at 84.2°F (29°C) for Hall (1988) for *T. teguixin* whereas Hurt (1995) reported 87 days at 84°F (28.6°C) for *T. rufescens*. Near the time of hatching, the eggs of Langerwerf's Argentine black and white tegus had increased somewhat in size and weight (one egg weighed 1.6 oz [45 g]!).

Hall (1978) noted that she kept her eggs in jars filled with sand on top of "small pea gravel." Water reached up to two-thirds the depth of the gravel. The jars were placed into an aquarium with a plastic lid and misted daily. Langerwerf (1995) places eggs in moist vermiculite at about 80 to 85°F (27 to 29°C), and they hatched in about 64 to 66 days. Hurt (1995) placed his *T. rufescens* eggs in moist vermiculite in a "Hovabator incubator" at 80 to 100% humidity.

Hatchling sizes reported by Hall (1978) were between 8.74 and 8.90 in. (22.2 and 22.6 cm) in TL, doubling in size within their first year (growth was asymmetrical, with the tail growing faster than the rest of the body). Hurt (1995, for *T. rufescens*) gave an average SVL for his hatchlings at 4 in. (10 cm) and an average TL at 9.5 in. (24.5 cm) whereas Langerwerf's black and white tegus averaged about 9.3 in. (23.7 cm) TL and 3.5 in. (9 cm) SVL. Luxmoore et al. (1988) reported hatchling sizes of about 7.5 to 7.9 in. (19 to 20 cm) in length, with the TL reaching about 13.8 in. (35 cm) in the first 5 months. Langerwerf (1992/93, 1995) observed that male Argentine black and white tegus may eat the eggs immediately after deposition and mentioned that gravid females attempt to find a secluded places to deposit them (Bayless [pers. comm.] claims this is true for savannah monitors as well). This is worth remembering when keeping several individuals housed together. Langerwerf's tegu laid her eggs in the soil, and he estimated the average temperature during incubation was about 82°F (27.6°C) and the incubation period was about 3 months. Ngo (pers. comm.) informed me that he gives gravid females 2.5 times the usual calcium supplement. His females lay their eggs in "sweater boxes" containing damp vermiculite, and these boxes are placed in a sheltered area.

Hall (1978) observed that newly hatched *T. teguixin* hatchlings molt in the first 2 hours after hatching! Hatchlings did not begin to feed until about 10 days old. However, she noted that they first ate earthworm sections dipped in egg yolk, and she postulates that they might begin feeding earlier if offered egg yolk. Later, they take baby mice and insects. She also described the defensive postures of the babies at 2 months old. They assume a bipedal stance with their forelegs held in the air and close to their bodies (similar to some monitor stances), and this is accompanied by loud hissing and open mouth threats. The posture is held for several seconds. She never observed adults do this. Langerwerf (1995) mentioned that his hatchlings would vibrate their tails like "colubrid snakes" when caught and handled.

Hurt (1995) observed his hatchling *T. rufescens* accept food within 24 hours. He fed them crickets and live pinkie mice daily during the first week of life and every second day thereafter. His hatchlings showed a "feeding frenzy," and he noted that limbs and tails are at some risk if the hatchlings are fed communally (Hurt 1995). At 9 months these hatchlings reached an average SVL of 7.5 in. (19 cm) and a TL of about 20 in. (51 cm). Hurt (1995) also noted that "their typical reddish adult colors became more obvious" at this time. He did not handle these hatchlings with any regularity to avoid "artificially taming" them.

Langerwerf (1995) reported that the fluid inside the egg squirts out as the baby emerges. In fact, he video recorded fluid squirting from an egg as far as 1 ft (0.3 m). He also noted that babies will emerge in less than 10 seconds and then make a quick dash for cover. Hurt (1995) claimed the baby red tegus "exploded" from the eggs when disturbed and that they are nervous, but Langerwerf (1995) claims this behavior occurs even without disturbance for Argentine black and white tegus and so believes it normal, at least for *T. teguixin*.

Appendix

Guidelines for the Keeping of Monitors and Tegus

Introduction

The following statement was drafted in response to the increasing number of proposals in part sponsored by anti-exotic-pet groups to restrict the rights of herpetoculturists to practice their avocation. A current trend among local animal control agencies has been to use arguments referring to "potential danger," or the biased arguments of organizations such as the Humane Society of America (HSA) (in their model regulations, HSA essentially states their opposition to the keeping of reptiles by the private sector), to attempt to implement a ban on the ownership of various reptiles. Large pythons, boas, and monitor lizards have increasingly become the target of these regulatory proposals.

Bias against the keeping of reptiles as pets

There has never been a recorded death of a human by a large monitor in the United States. There have also been very few injuries ever reported. In fact, in many townships or counties where regulations restricting the ownership of monitors have been proposed and/or passed (i.e., San Diego County and San Diego City, CA) the respective animal control agencies usually don't have a single case on record of a complaint or bite involving a monitor lizard or any other lizard. The same cannot be said of the domestic dog which kills 10 to 15 people a year or of the domestic horse which kills an even greater number of people. Furthermore, millions of dollars are spent every year in treating dog bites, cat bites, and injuries caused by horses. Remember, too, that it is not possible for any reptile to ever contract rabies! Certainly, many other things in everyday life constitute a greater threat than reptiles, such as automobiles, electrical appliances, cooking gas, alcohol, tobacco, firearms, and sometimes, unfortunately, our fellow human beings. What becomes evident is that regulatory agencies can be discriminatory and biased when it comes to what citizens of the United States can keep as pets. Many of these agencies perpetuate misinformation and a prejudice against reptiles. The constitutionality of such regulations has at least been questioned in one legal case in the state of Michigan.

What are the real potential dangers presented by monitor lizards?

Large monitor lizards (see section: An overview of monitors sold in the pet trade) can, if handled inappropriately, inflict painful and even possibly serious injuries as a result of scratches by their well-developed claws and in some circumstances as a result of bites inflicted by their powerful jaws. Bites by large monitors can under certain circumstances result in injuries requiring stitches, may result in infections, and, under extremely rare circumstances, can result in more serious injuries. Such incidents are rare because monitors typically avoid confrontation and seek flight. They will bite usually when maintained or handled in an inappropriate manner. Virtually all serious injuries reported (very few) in the United States were inflicted on herpetoculturists or prospective owners practicing poor maintenance or handling procedures.

Typically, when cornered, all monitors first thrash and strike out with their powerful tails to avoid confrontation—normally with substantial hissing and puffing. These tail strikes can result in superficial welts. Escaped larger monitors pose relatively little threat to humans. However, they could pose a threat to small domesticated animals that would be perceived as potential prey. Because of the relatively small number of escaped monitors, such a threat is in fact very small and virtually insignificant compared to the havoc wreaked on native wildlife and pets by the hordes of domestic cats which routinely roam free in most areas inhabited by humans in the United States.

As a whole, available data do not suggest that monitor lizards are of significant medical concern compared to many of the other domestic pets and animals routinely owned by human beings.

AFH Guidelines for Responsible Monitor Ownership

At the onset, the American Federation of Herpetoculturists (AFH) feels it is unnecessary to establish a permit system for keeping monitor lizards because these animals are not usually an animal control problem. Nonetheless, out of consideration for the animals, for family members, and for members of the general public, the AFH recommends the following guidelines for the keeping of monitor lizards. Acting as responsible herpetoculturists and pet owners can only help protect our rights to continue to practice our avocation.

1. All monitor lizards, and particularly species that can grow to an adult length of 4 feet or more (e.g., *Varanus exanthematicus*, *V. niloticus*, *V. salvator* of the pet trade), should be kept in escape-proof cages with a sliding top or sliding front or hinged top or hinged front doors with a locking mechanism. These recommendations are made to prevent inadvertent exposure of members of the public to these lizards and to prevent the occasional escape of pet monitors (the state of Florida appears to be No. 1 in terms of reports of escaped reptiles, including monitors). These escape incidents reflect poorly on private herpetoculturists, and this is the primary reason for recommending these cage regulations. Simple regulations by local agencies that require caging standards for housing large reptiles can help establish responsible herpetoculture that protects public welfare as well as the welfare of the animals.

2. The AFH recommends all monitors be transported in a manner that precludes escape: In a sturdy cloth bag free of holes or tears which is then placed inside a box or similar container with holes for aeration. The box or container should then be locked or sealed shut. Care must be taken to use sturdy cloth bags with a weave that allows for adequate air flow. An alternative to the above is to transport monitors in specially designed wood enclosures (with wire and or holes for air flow) with a hinged lid or door which should be securely locked. Cages sold for shipping or transporting dogs on airlines are also suitable for transporting large monitors.

3. No minors should be allowed to own monitor lizards without the parental consent to assume responsibility for proper housing, care, and supervision when handling.

Protection: All monitor lizards are listed as Appendix II (threatened) animals by CITES and therefore require permits for import\export between countries. The following species are listed under **Appendix I (endangered):** *Varanus bengalensis*, *V. flavescens*, *V. griseus*, and *V. komodoensis*. These endangered species are also protected under the Endangered Species Act.

155

4. When handling monitor lizards over 4 feet in length, the AFH recommends that another person be present for assistance or at least within shouting distance.

5. Out of consideration for those members of the public who may have a "phobia" about reptiles, monitor lizards should not be openly displayed in a public setting outside of a proper forum, such as educational demonstrations and shows, herpetological events and shows, and in pet stores.

6. Some monitors are listed as endangered under CITES Appendix I and the Endangered Species Act. The required paperwork should be in the possession of the owner to prove legal origin of captive.

7. As with other animals, such as dogs, owners of large monitors should remember that they can be liable for the medical costs of treating injuries as well as additional financial damages for traumas or damage caused by their animals.

8. As with all other nonnative wildlife, no monitor lizards should be intentionally released into the wild. Unwanted monitor lizards should be donated or offered for sale either through advertisement or through contacting dealers, herpetological societies, or zoos.

An Overview of Monitors Commonly Sold in the Pet Trade

At the time of writing, the most commonly sold monitors in the pet trade are the African "savannah" monitor (*Varanus exanthematicus* or *V. albigularis*) and the African Nile monitor (*V. niloticus*). As a rule, "savannah" monitors grow moderately large (3.5 to 5 feet, occasionally larger, depending on species or country of origin), adapt well to captivity, and, when raised from young animals and regularly handled, tend to become quite tame.

Nile monitors also adapt well to captivity, grow relatively large (4 to 7 feet, depending on variety and country of origin), but frequently remain nervous. They do not typically become as docile as "savannah" or water monitors, but may become remarkably tame under the right conditions.

Other monitors sold in significant numbers in the pet trade include the Asian water monitor (*V. Salvator*), which grows to 5 to 8 feet. These large monitors when raised from young animals and regularly handled are among the most docile of the monitors. On the other hand, imported adults of this species can be very difficult to handle and aggressive when defending themselves. Nonetheless, Asian water monitors are one of the most intelligent lizards, and this feature along with their large size and tendency toward docility make them very popular among fanciers of large monitors. A few other monitor species regularly available in small numbers in the pet trade include Dumeril's monitors (*V. dumerilii*), black rough-necked monitors (*V. Rudicollis*), and mangrove monitors (*V. indicus*). These are moderately large and relatively easy to manage species. They present no special problems in handling.

Other monitors imported in small numbers in recent years include rare Australasian species (*V. prasinus* spp., *V. timorensis*, *V. salvadorii*, and *V. gouldii*). Only the Papuan monitor (*V. salvadorii*), because of its large size (this is the second largest species of lizard) and relatively large teeth, warrant special precautions and housing as mentioned in these guidelines. These large monitors have been imported in very small numbers and sold at very high prices, which has effectively restricted their ownership to the more specialized and experienced collectors. The relative rarity of these in herpetoculture currently doesn't warrant any special local regulations for ownership other than the guidelines mentioned above.

These Guidelines have been approved by the American Federation of Herpetoculturist's (AFH) Board of Directors as the official *Guidelines for the Keeping of Monitor Lizards*. Additional copies of these guidelines are available by writing the AFH, P.O. Box 300067, Escondido, CA 92030-0067. [Note: the above is a slight modification of the guidelines published by the AFH in their legislative packet]

Acknowledgments: The AFH would like to thank the individuals involved in the preparation and successful completion of these guidelines: Michael Balsai, Philippe de Vosjoli, Greg Naclerio, and Robert Sprackland.

Source Materials

Acharijyo, L. N., and S. Mobapatra. 1989. Eggs of the water monitor (*Varanus salvator*) laid in captivity. *Indian Forester* 106(3): 230.

Alberts, A. 1994a. Ultraviolet light and lizards: More than meets the eye. *The Vivarium* 5(1): 24–25.

———. 1994b. Off to see the lizard: Lessons from the wild. *The Vivarium* 5(5): 26–28.

Alden, P. C., R. E. Estes, D. Schlitter, and B. McBride. 1995. *National Audubon Society Field Guide to African Wildlife*. Knopf, New York. 988 p.

Allen, M. E., and O. T. Oftedal. 1989. Dietary manipulation of the calcium content of feed crickets. *Journal of Zoo and Wildlife Medicine* 20(1): 26–33.

———. 1994. The nutrition of carnivorous reptiles. In: Murphy, J. B., K. Adler, and J. T. Collins (eds). *Captive Management and Conservation of Amphibians and Reptiles*. Society for the Study of Reptiles and Amphibians, Ithaca, NY. *Contributions to Herpetology*, Vol. 11. p. 71–82.

Andrews, H. 1991. *Varanus salvator*. VaraNews 1(6): 4.

———. 1995. Sexual maturation in *Varanus salvator* (Laurenti, 1768) with notes on growth and reproductive effort. *Herpetological Journal* 5: 189–194.

Anonymous. 1978. *Varanus salvator* breeding at Madras Snake Park. *Hamadryad* 3(2): 4.

Anonymous. 1984. CITES: *Convention on International Trade in Endangered Species of Wild Fauna and Flora* (50 CFR 23.23). U.S. Fish and Wildlife Service, U. S. Department of the Interior. 30 p.

Anonymous. 1993. *American Federation of Herpetoculturists Legislative Packet*. AFH, Escondido, CA. 8 sections (pages numbered accordingly).

Anonymous. 1993. Brest van Kempen wins. *Reptile & Amphibian Magazine* September–October 1993: 45–47.

Anonymous. 1994. *1994 Proceedings of the Association of Reptilian & Amphibian Veterinarians*. Association of Reptilian & Amphibian Veterinarians (A.R.A.V.), Chester Heights, PA. 121 p.

Arena, P. C., and C. Warwick. 1995. Miscellanous factors affecting health and welfare. In: Warwick, C., F. L. Frye, and J. B. Murphy (eds). *Health and Welfare of Captive Reptiles*. Chapman & Hall, London. p. 263–283.

Attum, O. 1994. A suggestion for controlling biting. *VaraNews* 4(2/3): 15.

Auffenberg, W. 1978. Social and feeding behavior in *Varanus komodoensis*. In: Greenberg, N., and P. D. MacLean (eds). *Behavior and Neurology of Lizards: An Interdisciplinary Colloquium*. National Institute of Mental Health, Rockville, MD. p. 301–331.

———. 1981. *The Behavioral Ecology of the Komodo Monitor*. University of Florida Press, Gainesville. 406 p.

———. 1983. Courtship behavior in *Varanus bengalensis* (Sauria: Varanidae). In: Rhodini, A. G. J., and K. Miyata (eds). *Advances in Herpetology and Evolutionary Biology: Essays in Honor of Ernest E. Williams*. Museum of Comparative Zoology, Harvard University, Cambridge, MA. p. 535–561.

———. 1988. *Gray's Monitor Lizard*. University of Florida Press, Gainesville. 419 p.

———. 1994. *The Bengal Monitor*. University of Florida Press, Gainesville. 560 p.

Avery, R. A. 1994. The effects of temperature on captive amphibians and reptiles. In: Murphy, J. B., K. Adler, and J. T. Collins (eds). *Captive Management and Conservation of Amphibians and Reptiles*. Society for the Study of Reptiles and Amphibians, Ithaca, NY. *Contributions to Herpetology*, Vol. 11. p. 47–51.

Balsai, M. J. 1990. Monitors: Dragons in captivity. *Reptile & Amphibian Magazine* July–August 1990: 2–5, 46–48.

———. 1991. Two wide ranging "Asian" Monitors. *VaraNews* 1(6): 57.

———. 1992. *The General Care and Maintenance of Savannah Monitors and Other Popular Monitor Species*. Advanced Vivarium Systems, Lakeside, CA 55 p.

———. 1993. Popular monitor species. *Reptiles* 1(2): 36–57.

————. 1995. Husbandry and breeding of the prehensile-tailed skink *Corucia zebrata*. *The Vivarium* 7(1): 4–11.

Balsai, M. J., and M. K. Bayless. 1993. Bizarre subcutaneous abscesses and possible causes in the savannah monitor lizard, *Varanus exanthematicus*. *VaraNews* 3(3): 7–10.

Barker, D. G. 1984. Maintenance and reproduction of green tree monitors at the Dallas Zoo. In: Hahn, R. A. (ed). *8th Annual Reptile Symposium on Captive Propagation & Husbandry*. Zoological Consortium Inc. Thurmont, MD. p. 91–92.

Barnard, S. M., and S. J. Upton. 1994. *A Veterinary Guide to the Parasites of Reptiles: Volume 1: Protozoa*. Krieger, Malabar, FL. 154 p.

Barten, S. L. 1992. How to buy a reptile. *Bulletin of the Chicago Herpetological Society* 27(9): 182–187.

————. 1996a. Reference sources for reptile clinicians. In: Mader, D. R. (ed). *Reptile Medicine and Surgery*. W. B. Saunders, Philadelphia. p. 33–38.

————. 1996b. Biology: Lizards. In: Mader, D. R. (ed). *Reptile Medicine and Surgery*. W. B. Saunders, Philadelphia. p. 47–61.

————. 1996c. Thermal burns. In: Mader, D. R. (ed). *Reptile Medicine and Surgery*. W. B. Saunders, Philadelphia. p. 419–421.

————. 1996d. Bites from prey. In: Mader, D. R. (ed). *Reptile Medicine and Surgery*. W. B. Saunders, Philadelphia. p. 353–355.

Barten, S. L., and R. A. Bennett. 1996. Treatment of chronic coxofemoral luxation by femoral head and neck excision arthroplasty in a white throated monitor, *Varanus albigularis*. *Bulletin of the Association of Reptilian and Amphibian Veterinarians* 6(1): 10–13.

Bayless, M. K. 1991. A trip to Africa. *VaraNews* 1(5): 5–8.

————. 1992a. Notes on the reproductive behavior of the Nile monitor lizard, *Varanus niloticus* Linnaeus (1766). *VaraNews* 2(4): 5–6.

————. 1992b African varanids: Diets in captivity and in the wild. *VaraNews* 2(5): 2–3.

————. 1992c. Reproductive notes on the black rough-neck monitor lizard (*Varanus rudicollis* Gray, 1845). *VaraNews* 3(2): 3.

————. 1994a. Zur Vortflanzungsbiologie des Steppenwarans (*Varanus exanthematicus*). *Salamandra*. 30(2): 109–118.

————. 1994b. The Papuan monitor lizard of New Guinea, *V. salvadorii*: Notes on its mystique. *VaraNews* 4(2/3): 6.

Bayless, M. K., and R. Huffaker 1992. Observations of egg deposition and hatching of the savannah monitor (*Varanus exanthematicus* Bosc, 1792) in captivity. *VaraNews* 3(1): 5–6.

Bayless, M. K., R. Huffaker, and O. Maercks. 1994. Notes on the egg deposition and incubation of the argus monitor (*Varanus gouldii horni*) Gray 1838) in captivity. *VaraNews* 4(1): 5.

Bayless, M. K., and T. Reynolds. 1992. Breeding of the savannah monitor lizard in captivity (*Varanus exanthematicus* Bosc, 1792). *Herpetology* 22(1): 12–14.

Behrmann, H. 1981 [1992]. Haltung und Nachzucht von *Varanus timorensis* [Care and reproduction of the Timor monitor, *Varanus timorensis*]. *Salamandra* 17(3/4): 198–201 [translation by Paul Gritis for *VaraNews* 2(6): 6].

Beltz, E. (ed). 1989. *Care in Captivity: Husbandry Techniques for Amphibians and Reptiles*. Chicago Herpetological Society, Chicago. 87 p.

Böhme, W. 1988. Zur Genitalmorphologie der Sauria: Funktionelle und stammesgeschichtliche Aspekte. *Bonner Zoologische Monographien* 27: 1–176.

————. 1991a. The identity of *Varanus gouldii* (Gray, 1838), and the nomenclature of the *V. gouldii* species complex. *Mertensiella* (Bonn, Germany) 2: 38–41.

————. 1991b. New findings on the hemipenial morphology of monitor lizards and their systematic implications. *Mertensiella* (Bonn, Germany) 2: 42–49.

————. 1995. Hemiclitoris discovered: a fully differentiated erectile structure in female monitor lizards (Varanus spp.) Reptilia: Varanidae *Journal of Zoological Syst. Evolutionary Research* 33: 129-132.

Böhme, W., and H. Horn (eds). 1991. Advances in monitor research. *Mertensiella* (Bonn, Germany) 2: 266 p.

Böhme, W., U. Joger, and B. Schätti. 1989. A new monitor lizard (Reptilia: Varanidae) from Yemen, with notes on ecology, phylogeny, and zoogeography. In: Buttiker, W., and F. Krupp (eds). *Fauna of Saudi Arabia*. Vol. 10. p. 433–448.

Böhme, W., H. Horn, and T. Ziegler. 1994. Zur taxonomie der Pazifikwarane (*Varanus-indicus*-Komplex): Revalidierung von *Varanus doreanus* (A.B. Meyer, 1874) mit Beschreibung einer neuen Unterart. *Salamandra* 30(2): 119–142.

Bowler, J. K. 1977. *Longevity of Reptiles and Amphibians in North American Collections*. Society for the Study of Amphibians and Reptiles and the Philadelphia Herpetological Society, Athens OH, 32 p.

Boyer, T. H. 1996. Metabolic bone disease. In: Mader, D. R. (ed). *Reptile Medicine and Surgery*. W. B. Saunders, Philadelphia. p. 385–392.

Boyer, D., and W. E. Lamoreaux 1983. Captive reproduction in the pygmy mulga monitor *Varanus gilleni* at the Dallas Zoo. In: Tolson, P. J. (ed). *7th. Annual Reptile Symposium on Captive Propagation & Husbandry*. Zoological Consortium Inc., Thurmont, MD. p. 59–63.

Boylan, T. 1995. Field observations, captive breeding and growth rates of the lace monitor, *Varanus varius*. *Herpetofauna* 25(1): 10–14.

Branch, W. R. 1982. Hemipeneal morphology of platynotan lizards. *Journal of Herpetology* 16(1): 16–38.

———. 1988. *Field Guide to the Snakes and other Reptiles of Southern Africa*. Ralph Curtis, Sanibel Island, FL. p. 326.

———. 1991. The Regenia Registers of Gogga Brown (1869–1909). "Memoranda on a species of monitor or varan." *Mertensiella* (Bonn, Germany) 2: 57–110.

Bredl, J., and T. D. Schwaner. 1983. First record of captive breeding of the lace monitor, *Varanus varius* (Sauria: Varanidae). *Herpetofauna* 15(1): 20–21.

Brown, R. W. 1956. *Composition of Scientific Words: A Manual of Methods and a Lexicon of Materials for the Practice of Logotechnics*. Smithsonian Institution Press, Washington, D.C. 882 p.

Burghardt, G. M., and D. Layne. 1995. Effects of ontogenetic processes and rearing conditions. In: Warwick, C., F. L. Frye, and J. B. Murphy (eds). 1995. *Health and Welfare of Captive Reptiles*. Chapman & Hall, London. p. 165–185.

Burghardt, G. M., and M. M. Milostan. 1995. Ethological studies on reptiles and amphibians: Lessons for species survival plans. In: Gibbons, E. F. Jr., B. S. Durrant, and J. Demarest (eds). *Conservation of Endangered Species in Captivity: An Interdisciplinary Approach*. State University of New York Press, Albany. p. 187–203.

Campbell, T. W. 1996. Hemoparasites. In: Mader, D. R. (ed). *Reptile Medicine and Surgery*. W. B. Saunders, Philadelphia. p. 379–381.

Card, W. 1993. Dallas Zoo reports significant monitor hatchings. *Communiqué* April 1993: 16.

———. 1994a. A reproductive history of monitors at the Dallas Zoo. *The Vivarium* 6(1): 26–29, 44–47.

———. 1994b Double clutching Gould's monitors (*Varanus gouldii*) and Gray's monitors (*Varanus olivaceus*) at the Dallas Zoo. *Herpetological Review* 25(3): 111–114.

———. 1994c. Emerald monitors. *Reptiles* 1(6): 4.

———. 1995a. Captive maintenance and reproduction of Gould's monitor lizard (*Varanus gouldii*). *Reptiles* 3(3): 84–91.

———. 1995b. Gray's monitor lizard (*Varanus olivaceus*) at the Dallas Zoo. *Reptiles* 3(5): 78–85.

Card, W. 1995c. Monitor lizard husbandry. *Bulletin of the Association of Reptilian and Amphibian Veterinarians* 5(3): 9–17.

Card, W., and A. G. Kluge. 1995. Hemipeneal skeleton and varanid systematics. *Journal of Herpetology* 29(2): 275–280.

Card, W., and D. Mehaffey 1994. A radiographic sexing technique for *Heloderma suspectum*. *Herpetological Review* 25(1): 17–19.

Carlzen, G. 1982. Breeding green tree monitors. *Herpetology Journal* 12(2): 4–6.

Carter, D. B. 1990. Courtship and mating in wild *Varanus varius* (Varanidae: Australia). *Memoranda of the Queensland Museum* 29(2): 333–338.

Cauble, C. 1992a. Routine laboratory tests for monitors. *VaraNews* 2(1): 7.

———. 1992b. Internal parasite detection. *VaraNews* 2(2): 7.

Chippindale, P. 1991. Captive breeding of the Timor monitor (*Varanus timorensis similis*) *Herpetological Review* 22(2): 52–53.

Chiszar, D., W. T. Tomlinson, H. M. Smith, J. B. Murphy, and C. W. Radcliffe. 1995. Behavioral consequences of husbandry manipulations: Indicators of arousal, quiescence and environmental awareness. In: Warwick, C., F. L. Frye, and J. B. Murphy (eds). *Health and Welfare of Captive Reptiles*. Chapman & Hall, London. p. 186–204.

Cissé, M. 1971. La diapause chez les Varanides du Senegal. *Notes Africaines* 131: 57–67 [translation in *VaraNews* 1994. 4(2/3): 7–11].

———. 1972. L' alimentation des Varanides au Senegal. *Bulletin de L'Institute Experimental d"Afrique Noire*. 34(2): 503–515 [translation in *VaraNews* 1992. 2(5): 3–6].

Cogger, H. G. 1992. *Reptiles and Amphibians of Australia*. (5th ed.) Cornell University Press, Ithaca, NY. p. 744.

Conners, S. 1994. Dumeril's monitor hatches at Birmingham Zoo. *Communiqué* December 1994: 24.

Cooper, J. E., and O. F. Jackson (eds). 1981. *Diseases of the Reptilia*, 2 volumes. Academic Press, London. 584 p.

Cooper, J. E., and D. L. Williams. 1995. Veterinary perspectives and techniques in husbandry and research. In: Warwick, C., F. L. Frye, and J. B. Murphy (eds). *Health and Welfare of Captive Reptiles*. Chapman & Hall, London. p. 98–112.

Cowan, D. F. 1980. Adaptation, maladaptation and disease. In: Murphy, J. B., and J. T. Collins (eds). *Reproductive Biology and Diseases in Captive Reptiles, SSAR Contributions to Herpetology no. 1*. Society for the Study of Amphibians and Reptiles, Ithaca, NY. p. 191–196.

Cowles, R. B. 1930. The life history of *Varanus niloticus* (Linnaeus) as observed in Natal South Africa. *Journal of Ent. Zoology* 22: 1–31.

Daltry, J. 1991. The social hierarchy of the water monitor, *Varanus salvator*. *Hamadryad* 16(1): 10–20.

Das, I. 1989. Indian monitor lizards: A review of human utilization patterns. *Hamadryad* 14: 16–19.

David, R. 1970. Breeding the mugger crocodile and water monitor *Crocodylus palustris* and *Varanus salvator* at the Ahmedabad Zoo. *International Zoo Yearbook* 10: p. 116–117.

Davis, R.B., and L. G. Phillips, Jr. 1991. A method of sexing the Dumeril's monitor. *Herpetological Review* 22(1): 18–19.

de Buffénil, V., C. Chabanet, and J. Castanet. 1994. Données préliminaires sur la taille, la croissance et la longévité du varan du Nil (*Varanus niloticus*) dans la région du lac Tchad. *Canadian Journal of Zoology* 72(2): 262–273.

DeNardo, D. 1990 Stress: A real but not well understood phenomenon. *The Vivarium* 2(5): 25–27, 29.

———. 1996 Reproductive biology. In: Mader, D. R. (ed). *Reptile Medicine and Surgery*. W. B. Saunders, Philadelphia. p. 212–224.

de Vosjoli, P. 1990. *The Right Way to Feed Insect-eating Lizards*. Advanced Vivarium Systems, Lakeside, CA. 32 p.

———. 1993. *The General Care and Maintenance of Prehensile-tailed Skinks*. Advanced Vivarium Systems, Lakeside, CA. 56 p.

———. 1994. *The Lizard Keeper's Handbook*. Advanced Vivarium Systems, Lakeside, CA. 175 p.

Ditmars, R. L. 1933. *Reptiles of the World*. Macmillian, New York. 321 p.

Done, L. B. 1996. Postural abnormalities. In: Mader, D. R. (ed). *Reptile Medicine and Surgery*. W. B. Saunders, Philadelphia. p. 406–411.

Donoghue, S., and J. Langenberg. 1996. Nutrition. In: Mader, D. R. (ed). *Reptile Medicine and Surgery*. W. B. Saunders, Philadelphia. p. 148–174.

Douglas, R. M. 1994 [1993]. High water potential Vermiculite as an incubation medium for reptile eggs. *Australian Herp News* May (#13): 4–8 [reprinted from: *British Herpetological Society Bulletin* #45, 1993].

Dryden, G., B. Green, D. King, and J. Losos. 1990. Water and turnover in a small monitor lizard, *Varanus acanthurus*. *Australian Wildlife Research* 17: 641–646.

Duvall D., L. J. Guillette, Jr., and R. E. Jones. 1982. Environmental control of reptilian reproductive cycles. In: Gans, C., and F. H. Pough (eds). *Biology of the Reptilia: Physiological Ecology*, Vol. 13, Physiology D. Academic Press, London. p. 201–271.

Eidenmüller, B. 1991. Zwillingsanlage bei *Varanus (varanus) mertensi* Glauert, 1951. *Salamandra* 27(4): 282–283.

———. 1992. Einige Bermerkungen über die Zeitgungsparameter von Warangelegen. *Monitor* 1(1): 14–20.

———. 1995. Successful breeding of Mertens' monitor lizard, *Varanus mertensi*. *The Vivarium* 7(2): 18–20.

Eidenmüller, B., and R. Wicker. 1995. The successful breeding of Mertens' monitor lizard, *Varanus mertensi*, Glauert 1951. *Herpetofauna* 25(2): 4–7.

Enright, B. 1992 [1989]. Notes on breeding the Nile monitor, *Varanus niloticus*, in captivity. *VaraNews* 2(6): 5 [reprinted from *Ontario Herp Society News*].

Erdelen, W. 1991. Conservation and population ecology of monitor lizards: The water monitor *Varanus salvator* (Laurenti, 1768) in South Sumatra. *Mertensiella* (Bonn, Germany) 2: 120–135.

Estes, R., K. De Queiroz, and J. Gauthier. 1988. Phylogenetic relationships within Squamata. In: Estes, R., and G. Pregill (eds). *Phylogenetic Relationships of the Lizard Families*, Stanford University Press, Stanford, CA. p. 119–281.

Ettling, J. 1992. Malayan water monitors hatch at the Sedgwick County Zoo & Botanical Gardens. *Communiqué* September 1992: 16.

Fagan, S. E. 1994. Taming the tumultuous tegu. *Behind BAARS* XVII (10): 1, 6.

Fitzgerald, L. A. 1994. *Tupinambis* lizards and people: A sustainable use approach to conservation and development. *Conservation Biology* 8(1): 12–16.

Fitzgerald, L. A., J. M. Chani, and O. C. Donadío. 1991. *Tupinambis* lizards in Argentina: Implementing management of a traditionally exploited resource. In: Robinson, J. G., and K. H. Redford (eds). *Neotropical Wildlife Use and Conservation*. University of Chicago Press, Chicago. p. 303–316.

Fitzgerald, L. A., F. B. Cruz, and G. Perotti. 1993. The reproductive cycle and the size at maturity of *Tupinambis rufescens* (Sauria: Teiidae) in the dry chaco of Argentina. *Journal of Herpetology*. 27(1): 70–78.

Fost, M. 1995. Dumeril's monitors hatched at Zoo Atlanta. *Communiqué* July 1995: 26.

Freer, N. 1993. Captive housing tips for a dumeril's monitor, *V. dumerilii*. *VaraNews* 3(4): 5.

Frost, M. 1992. Acquiring a new monitor: Purchase & parasite prevention. *VaraNews* 3(6): 1–2.

Frye, F. L. 1991. *Biomedical and Surgical Aspects of Captive Reptile Husbandry*, Vols. 1 and 2. Krieger, Malabar, FL. p. 345–392.

———. 1995. Nutritional considerations. In: Warwick, C., F. L. Frye, and J. B. Murphy (eds). *Health and Welfare of Captive Reptiles*. Chapman & Hall, London. p. 82–97.

Fulbeck, J. 1947. Monitors in the Marshalls. *Fauna* 9(4): 122–124.

Funk, R. S. 1996a. Anorexia. In: Mader, D. R. (ed). *Reptile Medicine and Surgery*, W. B. Saunders, Philadelphia. p. 346–348.

———. 1996b. Diarrhea. In: Mader, D. R. (ed). *Reptile Medicine and Surgery*. W. B. Saunders, Philadelphia. p. 364–365.

Funk, R. S., and P. R. Vilaro. 1980. An English translation of Robert Mertens' Keys to the monitor lizards, with a list of currently recognized species and subspecies. *Bulletin of the Chicago Herpetological Society* 15(2): 31–46.

Gans, C., and D. Crews (eds). 1992. *Hormones, Brain, and Behavior: Biology of the Reptilia*, Vol. 18, Physiology E. University of Chicago Press, Chicago. 564 p.

Garrett, C. M., and M. C. Peterson. 1991. *Varanus prasinus beccarii* behavior. *Herpetological Review* 22(3): 99–100.

Gaulke, M. 1991. On the diet of the water monitor, *Varanus salvator*, in the Philippines. *Mertensiella* (Bonn, Germany) 2: 143–153.

Gehrmann, W. H. 1987. Ultraviolet irradiances of various lamps used in animal husbandry. *Zoo Biology* 6: 117–127.

———. 1994a. Spectral characteristics of lamps commonly used in herpetoculture. *The Vivarium* 5(5): 16–21, 29.

———. 1994b. Light requirements of captive amphibians and reptiles. In: Murphy, J. B., K. Adler. and J. T. Collins (eds). *Captive Management and Conservation of Amphibians and Reptiles*. Society for the Study of Reptiles and Amphibians, Ithaca, NY. *Contributions to Herpetology*, Vol. 11. p. 53–59.

———. 1996 Evaluation of artificial lighting. In: Mader, D. R. (ed). *Reptile Medicine and Surgery*. W. B. Saunders, Philadelphia. p. 463–465.

Gehrmann, W. H., G. W. Ferguson, T. W. Odom, D. T. Roberts, and W. J. Barcellona. 1991. Early growth and bone mineralization of the iguanid lizard, *Sceloporus occidentalis* in captivity: Is vitamin D₃ supplementation or ultraviolet B irradiation necessary? *Zoo Biology* 10: 409–416.

Gibbons, E. E. Jr., et al. (eds). 1994 *Naturalistic Environments in Captivity for Animal Behavior Research*. State University of New York Press, Albany. 387 p.

Gillingham, J. C. 1995. Normal behavior. In: Warwick, C., F. L. Frye, and J. B. Murphy (eds). *Health and Welfare of Captive Reptiles*. Chapman & Hall, London. p. 131–164.

Gorman, D. 1993. Breeding the Bengal monitor in captivity. *VaraNews* 3(4): 2.

Gotch, A. F. 1986. *Reptiles: Their Latin Names Explained*. Blandford Press, Poole, Dorset, England. 176 p.

Greek, T. J. 1991. Operative temperature for the herpetoculturist. In: Staub, R. E. (ed). *Captive Propagation and Husbandry of Reptiles and Amphibians 1991*. Northern California Herpetological Society, Special Publication #6. p. 91–95.

Green, B., and D. King. 1993. *Goanna: The Biology of Varanid Lizards*. New South Wales University Press, Kensington, NSW, Australia. p. 102.

Greenberg, N. 1995. Ethologically informed design in husbandry and research. In: Warwick, C., F. L. Frye, and J. B. Murphy (eds). 1995. *Health and Welfare of Captive Reptiles*. Chapman & Hall, London. p. 239–262.

Greer, A. E. 1989. *The Biology & Evolution of Australian Lizards*. Surrey Beatty & Sons Pty Limited, NSW, Australia. p. 264.

Gregory, P. T. 1982. Reptilian hibernation. In: Gans, C., and F. H. Pough (eds). *Biology of the Reptilia: Physiological Ecology*, Vol. 13, Physiology D. Academic Press, London. p. 53–154.

Guillette, L. J. Jr., A. Cree, and A. A. Rooney. 1995. Biology of stress: interactions with reproduction, immunology and intermediary metabolism. In: Warwick, C., F. L. Frye, and J. B. Murphy (eds).. *Health and Welfare of Captive Reptiles*. Chapman & Hall, London. p. 32–81.

Haacke, W. D. 1995. Varanidae: *Varanus niloticus niloticus,* Nile monitor: Size. *African Herp News March 1995* 22: 45–46.

Haagner, G. V., R. J. Hall, and W. R. Branch. 1993. Nile monitor notes from South Africa. *VaraNews* 3(6): 4.

Hairston, C. S., and P. M. Burchfield. 1992. The reproduction and husbandry of the water monitor (*Varanus salvator*) at the Gladys Porter Zoo, Brownsville. *International Zoo Yearbook* 31: 124–130.

Hall, B. J. 1978. Notes on the husbandry, behavior and breeding of captive tegu lizards. *International Zoo Yearbook* 18: 91–95.

Halliday, T. R., and K. Adler. 1986. *All the World's Animals: Reptiles and Amphibians*. Torstar Books, New York. 160 p.

Hediger, H. 1985. A lifelong attempt to understand animals. In: Drewsbury, D. A. (ed). *Studying Animal Behavior: Autobiographies of the Founders*. University of Chicago Press, Chicago. p. 145–181.

Holmes, R. S., et al. 1975. Phenetic relationships among varanid lizards based upon comparative electrophoretic data and karyotypic analysis. *Biochemical System. Ecology* 3: 257–262.

Honegger, R. E. 1975. Breeding and maintaining reptiles in captivity. In: Martin, R. D. (ed). *Breeding Endangered Species in Captivity*. Academic Press, New York. p. 1–12.

Horn, H. 1991. Breeding of the lace monitor (*Varanus varius*) for the 1st time outside of Australia (Reptilia: Sauria: Varanidae) *Mertensiella* (Bonn, Germany) 2: 168–175.

Horn, H., and G. J. Visser. 1989. Review of reproduction of monitor lizards *Varanus* spp. in captivity. *International Zoo Yearbook* 28: 140–150.

———. 1991. Basic data on the biology of monitors. *Mertensiella* (Bonn, Germany) 2: 176–187.

Horn, H., M. Gaulke, and W. Böhme. 1994. New data on ritualized combats in monitor lizards (Sauria: Varanidae), with remarks on their function and phylogenetic implications. *Zool. Garten N. F.* 64(5): 265–280.

Hoogmoed, M. S., and J. Lescure. 1975. An annotated checklist of the lizards of French Guiana, mainly based on two recent collections. *Zoologische Mededelingen* 49(13): 141–172.

Hoser, R. T. 1989. *Australian Reptiles & Frogs.* Pierson & Co., Sydney, Australia. 238 p.

Hubert, J. 1985. Embryology of the squamata. In: Gans, C., and F. Billett (eds). *Biology of the Reptilia*, Vol. 15, Development B. John Wiley, New York. p. 1–34.

Hurt, C. 1995. The red tegu: Notes on captive breeding. *Reptiles*. 3(1): 80–89.

Inskipp, T. 1982. World trade in monitor lizard skins, 1977–1982. *Traffic Bulletin* VI(3/4): 51–53.

Inskipp, T. 1981. *Indian Trade in Reptile Skin.* Conservation Monitoring Centre, Cambridge, UK. p. 13.

Irwin, B. 1986 [1991]. Captive breeding success: *Varanus mertensi, Varanus gouldii. Thylacinus* 11(2): [*VaraNews* 1(7): 6–7].

Jacobson, E. R., and G. V. Kolias (eds). 1988. *Exotic Animals.* Churchill Livingstone, New York. 328 p.

James, C. D., J. B. Losos, and D. R. King. 1992. Reproductive biology and diets of goannas (Reptilia: Varanidae) *Australian Journal of Herpetology* 26(2): 128–136.

King, D., and B. Green. 1979. Notes on diet and reproduction of the sand goanna *Varanus gouldii rosenbergii. Copeia* 1979(1): 64–70.

King, D., and L. Rhodes. 1982. Sex ratio and breeding season of *Varanus acanthurus. Copeia* 1982(4): 784–787.

King, M. 1990. Chromosomal and immunogenetic data: A new perspective on the origin of Australia's reptiles. In: Olmo, E. (ed). *Cytogenetics of Amphibians and Reptiles.* Birkhauser Verlag, Basel, Switzerland. p. 153–180.

King, M., and D. King. 1975. Chromosomal evolution in the lizard genus *Varanus* (Reptilia). *Australian Journal of the Biological Sciences* 28: 89–108.

Klingenberg, R. J. 1993. *Understanding Reptile Parasites: A Basic Manual for Herpetoculturists and Veterinarians.* Advanced Vivarium Systems, Lakeside, CA. 81 p.

———. 1996a. Therapeutics. In: Mader, D. R. (ed). *Reptile Medicine and Surgery.* W. B. Saunders, Philadelphia. p. 299–321.

———. 1996b. Enteric cryptosporidiosis in a colony of indigo snakes *Drymarchon corais* spp., a panther chameleon, *Chamaeleo pardalis*, and a savannah monitor, *Varanus exanthemanticus. Bulletin of the Association of Reptilian and Amphibian Veterinarians* 6(1): 5–9.

Krebs, U. 1979. Der Duméril-Waran (*Varanus dumerilii*), ein spezialisierter Krabbenfresser? *Salamandra* 15(3): 146–157.

Kukol, Z. 1993. Captive *V. indicus* egg deposition. *VaraNews* 3(3): 5.

Lane, T. J., and D. R. Mader. 1996. Parasitology. In: Mader, D. R. (ed). *Reptile Medicine and Surgery.* W. B. Saunders, Philadelphia. p. 185–203.

Lange, J. 1989. Observations on the Komodo monitors in the Zoo-Aquarium Berlin. *International Zoo Yearbook* 28: 151–153.

Langerwerf, B. 1992/93. The reproduction of the Argentine black and white tegu, *Tupinambis teguixin*, in captivity. *British Herpetological Society Bulletin* 42: 18–23.

———. 1995. Keeping and breeding the Argentine black and white tegu, *Tupinambis teguixin. The Vivarium* 7(3): 24–29.

Laurent, R. F. 1964. A new subspecies of *Varanus exanthematicus* (Sauria, Varanidae). *Breviora* (199): 1–9.

————. 1979. Herpetofaunal relationships between Africa and South America. In: Duellman, W. E. (ed). *The South American Herpetofauna: Its Origin, Evolution, and Dispersal*. Museum of Natural History, The University of Kansas Monograph No. 7, p. 55–71.

Lawrence, E. 1989. *Henderson's Dictionary of Biological Terms*. John Wiley, New York. 637 p.

Lawton, M. P. C. 1991. Reptiles part two: Lizards and snakes. In: Beynon, P. H., and J. E. Cooper (eds). *Manual of Exotic Pets*. Iowa State University Press, Ames. p. 244–260.

Lemm, J. 1994. Captive husbandry of white-throated monitors (*Varanus albigularis*) at the San Diego Zoo's Center for Reproduction of Endangered Species (C.R.E.S.). *VaraNews* 4(2/3): 4–5.

Licht, P. 1995. Reproductive physiology of reptiles and amphibians: Lessons for survival plans. In: Gibbons, E. F. Jr., B. S. Durrant, and J. Demarest (eds). *Conservation of Endangered Species in Captivity: An Interdisciplinary Approach*. State University of New York Press, Albany. p. 169–186.

Lillywhite, H. B., and R. E. Gatten, Jr. 1995. Physiology and functional anatomy. In: Warwick, C., F. L. Frye, and J. B. Murphy (eds). 1995. *Health and Welfare of Captive Reptiles*. Chapman & Hall, London. p. 5–31.

Limpus, D. J. 1995. Observations of *Varanus gouldii* (Varanidae) at Mon Repos Beach Bundaberg. *Herpetofauna* 25(2): 14–16.

Losos, J. B, and H. W. Greene. 1988. Ecological and evolutionary implications of diet in monitor lizards. *Biological Journal of the Linnean Society* 35: 379–407.

Luxmoore, R., and B. Groombridge. 1989. *Asian Monitor Lizards: A Review of Distribution, Status, Exploitation and Trade in Four Selected Species*. (Draft Report to CITES Secretariat). World Conservation Monitoring Centre. Cambridge, UK. 190 p.

Luxmoore, R., B. Groombridge, and S. Broad (eds). 1988. *Significant Trade in Wildlife: A Review of Selected Species in CITE'S Appendix II. Volume 2: Reptiles and Invertebrates*. International Union for Conservation of Nature and Natural Resources. Cambridge, UK. 306 p.

Mader, D. R. 1993. Mite and tick infestions. *Reptiles* 1(1): 64–72.

————. 1994. Reptile endoparasites. *Reptiles* 1(4): 64–71.

————. 1996. Acariasis. In: Mader, D. R. (ed). *Reptile Medicine and Surgery*. W. B. Saunders, Philadelphia. p. 341–346.

McCoid, M. J. 1993. Reproductive output of captive and wild mangrove monitors (*Varanus indicus*). *VaraNews* 3(3): 4–5.

McCoid, M. J., and R. A. Hensley. 1991. Mating and combat in *Varanus indicus*. *Herp. Review*. 22(1): 16–17.

————. 1993. Observations of *Varanus indicus* in the Mariana Islands. *VaraNews* 3(6): 4–5.

McCoid, M. J., R. A. Hensley, and G. J. Witteman. 1994. Factors in the decline of *Varanus indicus* on Guam, Mariana Islands. *Herpetoloical Review* 25(2): 60–61.

McCoid, M. J., and G. J. Witteman. 1993. *Varanus indicus* (mangrove monitor) diet. *Herpetological Review* 24(3): 105.

McGinnity, Dale. 1993. Captive notes on 3 *V. rudicollis* at the Nashville Zoo. *VaraNews* 3(6): 2.

McKeown, S. 1996. General husbandry and management. In: Mader, D. R. (ed). *Reptile Medicine and Surgery* W. B. Saunders, Philadelphia. p. 9–19.

Maixner, J. M., E. C. Ramsay, and L. H. Arp. 1987. Effects of feeding on serum uric acid levels in captive reptiles. *Journal of Zoo Animal Medicine* 18: 62–65.

Marcus, L. C. 1981. *Veterinary Biology and Medicine of Captive Amphibians and Reptiles*. Lea & Febiger, Philadelphia. 239 p.

Markwell, K. 1983. The artificial incubation of lace monitor (*Varanus varius*) eggs. *Herpetofauna* 15(1): 16–17.

Martuscelli, P., and F. Olmos. 1996. *Tupinambis teguixin* (common tegu) foraging. *Herpetological Review* 27(1): 21.

Mercolli, C., and A. Yanosky. 1994. The diet of adult *Tupinambis teguixin* (Sauria: Teiidae) in the eastern Chaco of Argentina. *Herpetological Journal* 4: 15–19.

Mertens, R. 1942. Die Familie der Warane *(Varanidae)*. *Abhandlungen der Senckenbergischen Naturforschenden Gesellschaft* 462: 1– 116; 465: 117–234; 466: 235–391.

———. 1950. Notes on some Indo-Australian monitors (Sauria: Varanidae) *American Museum Novitates* 1456: 1–7.

———. 1963. Liste der rezenten Amphibien und Reptilien. Helodermatidae, Varanidae, Lanthanontidae. *Das Tierreich, Berlin* 79: i–x = 1–26.

———. 1962. *Papusaurus*, eine neue Untergattung von *Varanus*. *Senkenbergiana Biologica* 42: 331–333.

McCoy, M. 1980. *Reptiles of the Solomon Islands: Wau Institute Handbook #7*. Wau, Papua, New Guinea. 80 p.

Miller, M. 1993. [Not titled]. *VaraNews* 3(4): 6.

Murphy, J. B. 1971. Notes on the care of the ridge-tailed monitor (*Varanus acanthurus brachyurus*) at the Dallas Zoo. *International Zoo Yearbook* 11: 230–231.

Murphy, J. 1972. Notes on Indo-Australian varanids in captivity. *International Zoo Yearbook* 12: 199–202.

Murphy, J. B., and J. Collins (eds). 1980. *Reproductive Biology and Diseases of Captive Reptiles*. Society for the Study of Amphibians and Reptiles, Ithaca, NY. *Contributions to Herpetology*, Vol. 1. 277 p.

Murphy, J. B., K. Adler, and J. T. Collins (eds). 1994 *Captive Management and Conservation of Amphibians and Reptiles*. Society for the Study of Reptiles and Amphibians, Ithaca, NY. *Contributions to Herpetology*, Vol. 11. 408 p.

Murray, M. J. 1996. Pneumonia and normal respiratory function. In: Mader, D. R. (ed). *Reptile Medicine and Surgery*. W. B. Saunders, Philadelphia. p. 396–405.

Naclerio, G. J. 1990. Inexpensive "water hole." *VaraNews* 1(0): 2–3.

———. 1993. Life with Nile monitors, *Varanus niloticus*: Part 1. *VaraNews* 3(5): 4–6.

Naclerio, G. J. 1994. Nile monitor anti-defamation league. *VaraNews* 4(2/3): 11–13.

Nelling, C. 1995. Mangrove monitors. *Reptile & Amphibian Magazine* January–February 1995: 30–35.

Norman, D. R. 1987. Man and tegu lizards in eastern Paraguay. *Biological Conservation* 41: 39–56.

O'Dell, J. 1992. Successful captive propagation of the freckled monitor (*Varanus tristis orientalis*). *VaraNews* 3(2): 4–6.

Olmo, E. 1986. Reptilia. In: Bernard, J. (ed). *Animal Cytogenetics* 4, Chordata 3. Berlin Gebrudes Borntrager, Berlin.

Olmos, F. 1995. *Tupinambis teguixin* (Tegu lizard): Aquatic behavior. *Herpetological Review* 26(1): 37.

Olson, W. 1992. Monitor medicine cabinet. *VaraNews* 2(2): 4.

Packard, G. C., and J. A. Phillips. 1994. The importance of the physical environment for the incubation of reptilian eggs. In: Murphy, J. B., K. Adler, and J. T. Collins (eds). *Captive Management and Conservation of Amphibians and Reptiles*. Society for the Study of Reptiles and Amphibians, Ithaca, NY. *Contributions to Herpetology*, Vol. 11. p. 195–208.

Patterson, R., and A. Bannister. 1987. *Reptiles of Southern Africa*. C. Struik, Capetown, South Africa. 128 p.

Patton, K. T. 1991. Understanding stress in captive reptiles. *The Vivarium* 2(6): 18, 36–7, 39.

Perry, G., R. Habani, and H. Mendelssohn. 1993. The first captive reproduction of the desert monitor (*Varanus griseus griseus*) at the Research Zoo of Tel Aviv University. *International Zoo Yearbook* 32: 188–190.

Perry-Peterson, J.J., and C.S. Ivanyi. 1995. Captive design for reptiles and amphibians. In: Gibbons, E. F. Jr., B. S. Durrant, and J. Demarest (eds). *Conservation of Endangered Species in Captivity: An Interdisciplinary Approach*. State University of New York Press, Albany. p. 205–221.

Peters, J. A., and R. Donoso-Barros. 1970 [1986]. *Catalogue of the Neotropical Squamata: Part II. Lizards and Amphisbaenians*. Bulletin of the U.S. National Museum 297: 1–293.

Pfaff, S. 1992. Riverbanks Zoo reports notable hatching. *Communiqué* February 1992: 12.

Phillips, J. A., and G. C. Packard. 1994. Influence of temperature and moisture on eggs and embryos of the white-throated savanna monitor *Varanus albigularis*: Implications for conservation. *Biological Conservation* 69(2): 131–136.

Presch, W. 1973. A review of the tegus, lizard genus *Tupinambis* (Sauria: Teiidae: Lacertilia). *Copeia* 1973(4): 740–746.

Radford, L., and F. L. Paine. 1989. The reproduction and management of the Dumeril's monitor. *International Zoo Yearbook* 28: 153–155.

Ramus, E. (ed). 1994. *1994–1995 Directory: A Guide to North American Herpetology. Reptile & Amphibian Magazine*, Pottsville, PA. 310 p.

Regal, P. J. 1980. Temperature and light requirements of captive reptiles. In: Murphy, J. B. and J. T. Collins (eds). *Reproductive Biology and Diseases of Captive Reptiles*. Society for the Study of Reptiles and Amphibians, Ithaca, NY. *Contributions to Herpetology*, Vol. 1. p. 79–89.

Rish, B. 1994. Komodo monitor eggs hatched at the Cincinnati Zoo. *Communiqué* April 1994: 12.

Roder, A., and H. Horn. 1994. Über zwei Nachzuchten des Steppenwarans (*Varanus exanthematicus*). *Salamandra* 30(2): 97–108.

Ross, R. A., and G. Marzec. 1984. *The Bacterial Diseases of Reptiles*. Institute for Herpetological Research. Stanford, CA.

———. 1990. *The Reproductive Husbandry of Pythons and Boas*. Institute for Herpetological Research. Stanford, CA. p. 270.

Rossi, J. V. 1992. *Snakes of the United States and Canada: Keeping Them Healthy in Captivity, Volume I, Eastern Area*. Krieger, Malabar, FL. 209 p.

———. 1996. Dermatology. In: Mader, D. R. (ed). *Reptile Medicine and Surgery*. W. B. Saunders, Philadelphia. p. 104–117.

Saint Girons, H. 1985. Comparative data on lepidosaurian reproduction and some time tables. In: *Biology of the Reptilia*, Vol. 15, Development B. John Wiley, New York. p. 35–58.

Schildger, B. 1987. Endoscopic sex determination in reptiles. *Proceedings of the First International Conference on Zoo and Avian Medicine*. p. 369–375.

Schildger, B., and R. Wicker. 1992. Endoscopie bei Reptilien und Amphibien— Indikationen, Methoden, Befunde. *Der praktische Tierarzt* 6: 517–526.

Shea, G. M., and G. L. Reddacliff. 1986. Ossifications in the hemipenes of varanids. *Journal of Herpetology* 20(4): 566–568.

Shine, R. 1986. Food habits, habitats, and reproductive biology of four sympatric species of varanid lizards in tropical Australia. *Herpetologica* 42(3): 346–360.

Slavens, F. L. 1989. *Reptiles and Amphibians in Captivity: Breeding—Longevity and Inventory*. Slaveware, Seattle, WA. 474 p.

Slavens, F. L., and K. Slavens. 1993. *Reptiles and Amphibians in Captivity: Breeding—Longevity and Inventory*. Slaveware, Seattle, WA. xx p.

Smeller, J. M., K. Slickers, and M. Bush. 1978. Effect of feeding on the plasma uric acid levels in snakes. *American Journal of Veterinary Research* 39(9): 1556–1557.

Smith, M. A. 1935. (Repr. 1973). *The Fauna of British India: Reptilia and Amphibia, Vol. 2: Sauria*. Ralph Curtis Books, Hollywood, FL. p. 440. [Reprint publisher]

Sprackland, R. G. 1989. Mating and waiting: A status report on reproduction in captive monitor lizards (Sauria: Varanidae). In: Gowen, R. L. (ed). *Captive Propagation and Husbandry of Reptiles and Amphibians 1989*. Northern California Herpetological Society, Special Publication #5. p. 57–63.

———. 1990. A preliminary study of food discrimination in monitor lizards (Reptilia: Lacertilia: Varanidae). *Bulletin of the Chicago Herpetological Society* 25(10): p. 181–183.

———. 1991a. A myriad of monitors. *Tropical Fish Hobbyist* January 1991: 130–138.

———. 1991b. The emerald tree monitor, *Varanus prasinus*. *Tropical Fish Hobbyist* January 1991: 110–114.

————. 1991c. Taxonomic review of the *Varanus prasinus* group with descriptions of two new species. *Memoranda of the Queensland Museum* 30(3): 561–576.

————. 1992. *Giant Lizards*. TFH Publications, Neptune City, NJ. p. 288.

————. 1993a. Rediscovery of a Solomon Islands monitor lizard (*Varanus indicus spinulosis*) Mertens, 1941. *The Vivarium* 4(5): 25–27.

————. 1993b. Etymology of varanid names. *VaraNews* 3(4): 3.

————. 1993c. The taxonomic status of the monitor lizard, *Varanus dumerilii hertopholis* Boulenger, 1892 (Reptilia: Varanidae). *Sawarak Museum Journal* XLIV(65): 113–121

————. 1994. Emerald monitors: Lean, green, and rarely seen. *Reptiles* 1(5): 16–23.

Staedeli, J. H. 1962. Our very own monitors. *Zoonooz* 35(7): 10–15.

Stahl, S. 1992. Monitor-ing medicine. *VaraNews* 2(3): 5–6.

Stewart, J. S. 1989. Techniques for sex identification in large reptiles. In: Gowen, R. L. (ed). *Captive Propagation and Husbandry of Captive Reptiles and Amphibians*. Northern California Herpetological Society, Special Publication #5. p. 57–63.

Storr, G. M. 1980. The monitor lizards (genus *Varanus* Merrem, 1820) of Western Australia. *Rec. Western Australian Museum, Perth*, 8(2): 273–293.

Storr, G. M., L. A. Smith, and R.E. Johnstone. 1983. *Lizards of Western Australia, Vol. 2: Dragons and Monitors*. Western Australian Museum, Belmont, Western Australia. p. 1 13.

Strimple, P. 1988. The savannah monitor, *Varanus exanthematicus* (Bosc, 1792). Part 1. *The Forked Tongue* 13(12): 8–13.

————. 1989a. The savannah monitor, *Varanus exanthematicus* (Bosc, 1792). Part 2. *The Forked Tongue* 14(l): 5–7.

————. 1989b. The savannah monitor, *Varanus exanthematicus* (Bosc, 1792). Part 3. *The Forked Tongue* 14(2): 5–8.

————. 1989c. The savannah monitor, *Varanus exanthematicus* (Bosc, 1792). Part 4. *The Forked Tongue* 14(3): 7–16.

————. 1989d. Observations on three captive juvenile West African savanna monitors, *Varanus e. exanthematicus* (Bosc, 1792). *Notes to NOAH* XVI(10): 8–12 [Reprinted in *VaraNews*. 1990. 1(2): 6–8].

————. 1996. Natural history and captive husbandry of selected monitor species. *Reptiles Annual 1996*: 136–153.

Strimple, P. D., and J. L. Strimple. 1996. Australia's largest goanna: The perentie. *Reptiles* 4(2): 76–87.

Surahya, S. 1989. *Komodo: Studi Anatomi dan kedudukannya Dalam Sistematik Hewan (An Anatomoical Study of the Komodo Dragon and its Position in Animal Systematics)*. Gadjah Mada University Press, Bulaksumur, Yogyakarta, Indonesia. p. 324. (Vol. 1) and 382 figures [*Atlas Komodo*] Vol. 2).

Swanson, S. 1987. *Lizards of Australia, Revised and Expanded Edition*. Angus & Robertson, North Ryde, Australia. 160 p.

Taylor, E. H. 1963. The lizards of Thailand. *University of Kansas Science Bulletin* LXIV: 687–1077.

Thissen, R. 1991. A double clutch and successful hatching of Australian spiney-tailed monitors, *Varanus acanthurus* Boulenger. *VaraNews* 1(7): 5–6.

————. 1992. Breeding the spiny-tail monitor (*Varanus acanthurus* Boulenger). *The Vivarium* 3(5): 32–34.

Thompson, G. 1992. Daily distance traveled and foraging areas of *Varanus gouldii* (Reptilia: Varanidae) in an urban environment. *Wildlife Research* 19(6): 743–753.

Turnipseed, J. 1995. Corrections and clarifications. *Iowa Herpetological Society News*. XVIII(5): 4.

Tyler, M. J. 1979. Herpetofaunal relationships of South America with Australia. In: Duellman, W. E. (ed). *The South American Herpetofauna: Its Origin, Evolution, and Dispersal*. Museum of Natural History, The University of Kansas Monograph No. 7, p. 73–106.

Uchida, T. A. 1966. Observations on the monitor lizard, *Varanus indicus* (Daudin), as a rat-control agent on Ifaluk, Western Caroline Islands. *Bulletin of the World Health Organization* 35: 976–980.

Valentic, R. 1994. The feeding strategy of *Varanus panoptes*, a field observation. *The Monitor* 6(2): 74.

van Kalken, C. 1993. Captive breeding success with the mangrove monitor. *VaraNews* 3(6): 2.

Visser, G. 1985 [1992]. Notizen zur Brutbiologie des Gelbwarans *Varanus (Empagusia) flavescens* (Hardwicke & Gray, 1827) im Zoo Rotterdam (Sauria Varanidae). [Notes on the breeding biology of the yellow monitor *Varanus (Empagusia) flavescens* (Hardwicke & Gray, 1827) in the Rotterdam Zoo. (Sauria Varanidae)]. *Salamandra* 21(2/3): 161–168 [Translated by Margaret Berker, edited by Ennis Berker, *VaraNews* 2(3): 2–5].

———. 1992. Monitors and the Rotterdam Zoo. *The Vivarium* 4(3): 19–22.

Vitt, L. J., and E. R. Pianka (eds). 1994. *Lizard Ecology: Historical and Experimental Perspectives*. Princeton University Press, Princeton, NJ. 403 p.

Walsh, T., and R. Rosscoe. 1992. National Zoo announces hatching of Komodo monitors. *Communiqué* December 1992: 17.

Walsh, T., R. Rosscoe, and G. F. Birchard. 1993. Dragon tales: The history, husbandry, and breeding of the Komodo monitors at the National Zoological Park. *The Vivarium* 4(6): 23–26.

Wanner, M. 1991. Black tree monitors hatch at the Fort Worth Zoo. *Communiqué* August 1991: 17.

Warwick, C. 1995. Psychological and behavioral principles and problems. In: Warwick, C., F. L. Frye, and J. B. Murphy (eds). *Health and Welfare of Captive Reptiles*. Chapman & Hall, London. p. 205–338.

Warwick, C., F. L. Frye, and J. B. Murphy (eds). 1995. *Health and Welfare of Captive Reptiles*. Chapman & Hall, London. 299 p.

Warwick, C., and C. Steedman. 1995. Naturalistic versus clinical environments in husbandry and research. In: Warwick, C., F. L. Frye, and J. B. Murphy (eds). *Health and Welfare of Captive Reptiles*. Chapman & Hall, London. p. 113–130.

Weigel, J. 1988. *Care of Australian Reptiles in Captivity*. Reptile Keepers Association, Gosford, NSW, Australia. 144 p.

Weldon, P. J., et al. 1994. Chemoreception in the feeding behavior of reptiles: Considerations for maintenance and management. In: Murphy, J. B., K. Adler, and J. T. Collins (eds). *Captive Management and Conservation of Amphibians and Reptiles*. Society for the Study of Reptiles and Amphibians, Ithaca, NY. *Contributions to Herpetology*, Vol. 11. p. 61–70.

Wesiak, K. 1992. Über einen bemerkenswerten Fall von Automutilation bei *Varanus acanthurus*. *Monitor* 1(1): 21–23.

———. 1993. Über Haltung und Nachzucht von *Varanus (Euprepiosaurus) indicus indicus* (Daudin, 1802). *Herpetofauna* 15(87): 21–25.

Whitaker, R., and Z. Whitaker. 1980. Distribution and status of *Varanus salvator* in India and Sri Lanka. *Herpetological Review* 11(3): 81–82.

Wilson, S. K., and D. G. Knowles. 1988. *Australia's Reptiles: A photographic Reference to the Terrestrial Reptiles of Australia*. Collins, Sydney, NSW, Australia. p. 447.

Wikramanayakae, E. D., and G. L. Dryden. 1988. The reproductive ecology of *Varanus indicus* on Guam. *Herpetologica* 44(3): 338–344.

Wise, M. A. 1994. Techniques for the capture and restraint of captive crocodilians. In: J. B. Murphy, K. Adler, and J. T. Collins (eds). *Captive Management and Conservation of Amphibians and Reptiles*. Society for the Study of Amphibians and Reptiles, Ithaca, NY. p. 401–405.

Wood, G. R. 1982. *The Guinness Book of Animal Facts and Feats, 3rd edition*. Guinness Superlatives, Ltd., Middlesex, England. 252 p.

Wright, K. 1993a. Suggested quarantine procedures for monitors and tegus. *The Vivarium* 5(3): 22–23.

———. 1993b Nile monitors. *Reptile & Amphibian Magazine* September–October 1993: 36–44.

———. 1993c. Disinfection for the herpetoculturist. *The Vivarium* 5(1): 31.

Wynne, R. H. 1981. *Lizards in Captivity*. TFH Publications, Neptune City, NJ. 189 p.

Zimmermann, E. 1986. *Breeding Terrarium Animals*. TFH Publications, Neptune City, NJ. 384 p.

Zwart, P., and R. J. Rulkens. 1979. Improving the calcium content of mealworms. *International Zoo Yearbook* 19: 254–255.

Index